MIRACLE
MATCH

Glory to G...
Sharon Ragsdale
Paul Ragsdale

MIRACLE MATCH

One Couple's Journey of Love, Survival, and Transplant

SHARON & PAUL RAGSDALE

TATE PUBLISHING
AND ENTERPRISES, LLC

This book is designed to provide accurate and authoritative information with regard to the subject matter covered. This information is given with the understanding that neither the author nor Tate Publishing, LLC is engaged in rendering legal, professional advice. Since the details of your situation are fact dependent, you should additionally seek the services of a competent professional.

The opinions expressed by the author are not necessarily those of Tate Publishing, LLC.

Published by Tate Publishing & Enterprises, LLC
127 E. Trade Center Terrace | Mustang, Oklahoma 73064 USA
1.888.361.9473 | www.tatepublishing.com

Tate Publishing is committed to excellence in the publishing industry. The company reflects the philosophy established by the founders, based on Psalm 68:11,
"The Lord gave the word and great was the company of those who published it."

Book design copyright © 2013 by Tate Publishing, LLC. All rights reserved.
Cover design by Rtor Maghuyop
Interior design by Honeylette Pino

Published in the United States of America

ISBN: 978-1-62563-847-2
1. Biography & Autobiography / General
2. Biography & Autobiography / Personal Memoirs
13.07.01

ACKNOWLEDGMENTS

Our story is a collective effort. We are definitely high maintenance and couldn't possibly list everyone, but there are some who simply must be acknowledged.

Our family has stuck by us through thick and thin, over and over. They are the following: parents John G. and DeDe Ragsdale and Jay and Faye Anderson; siblings Julia Lovorn, Kathryn (and Gary) Valentine, David (and Judy) Ragsdale, Cynthia (and Dennis) DeLaughter, and Milton (and Deme) Anderson; and children Jason Webb, Kristen (and Jason) Jackson, Cindy (and Rett) Rabe, and Lindsay Ragsdale. Ray DeLaughter knows how to sit quietly in a hospital room. Rachel Bosworth contributed valuable editing insight.

Friends and family have been faithful prayer warriors. Their tenacity cannot be overstated, and we are wholly in their debt: Tim Black, Joy Lasco, Raymond Jackson, Bruce Plummer, Larry and Sylvia Walls, John and Susie Pipkin, Bob and Shirley Skiebe, Wade and Debbie Norman.

From Houston's First Baptist Church: John Bolin, His Glory class, and the choir and orchestra. Metropolitan Baptist Church friends persistently prayed.

St. Luke's Episcopal Hospital physicians Dr. Victor Narcisse, Dr. Alberto Colomer, Dr. Sayed Feghali, Dr. Risë Stribling, Dr. Juan Gonzalez, Dr. Christine O'Mahony, and physician assistant Debbie Calaris were critical to Paul's survival in November 2011.

Kidney transplant group members Dr. Charles Van Buren, Dr. Jacqueline Lappin, Dr. Stephen Katz, Dr. Debra Doherty, physician assistant Barbi Witz, *and their entire team*, were instrumental in successful kidney surgeries. Thank you.

Current Cypress Assisted Living staff includes Angie Babauta, Jennifer Smith, Veronique Ngo Ndoum, Aida Sibal, Dulce Villalba, Honoree Bassognyam, Dominique Holmes, Sara Matheson, and Marisol Cortez. They are amazing!

Heartfelt appreciation is extended to all organ donors as well as to families who have permitted donation from deceased loved ones. Please consider this gift of life and notify key family members of your decision. It really is so important.

Above all is our Lord and Savior Jesus Christ, who redeemed us from a life of uncertainty and made joy and hope an everlasting reality. All praise is his!

CONTENTS

Part Three: Transplant

PREFACE

This is a true story about real people. Against all odds, God matched our lives and our kidneys. This book tells the story that was too amazing to keep to ourselves.

Our goals were:

- To give God the glory and
- To encourage future kidney donors.

Our story cannot be told without medical discussion because Paul's struggles and miracles often revolve around it. We hope it serves as clarification. Sharon is the primary author; Paul's comments are in italics. We hope you enjoy our story!

With love,
Sharon and Paul Ragsdale

PART ONE:
OUR BEGINNING

ONE SMALL SIP

It all started with a sip of soda. November 1, 2011 was just a regular day. My husband Paul and I were watching TV that evening, and he drank some Diet Coke. It went down the wrong way, and he started coughing. And coughing. He couldn't stop coughing even through the night. It was worrisome, but he was okay, except for that persistent cough.

Let me back up a little bit because unfortunately, insignificant events often spell big trouble for Paul. Although he looks like a regular guy, Paul has a long and complicated medical history. A diagnosis of Crohn's disease in his mid-twenties set the stage for lifelong challenges and multiple organ complications.

Crohn's disease is a chronic, inflammatory disease that can affect any portion of the gastrointestinal (GI) tract. Symptoms include persistent diarrhea, bleeding, abdominal pain, weight loss, and fatigue. Frequent flare-ups and remissions are common. Even with treatment, up to 70 percent of Crohn's patients require surgery to remove portions of the affected GI tract, which provides a higher quality of life.[1] Paul eventually fell into this category.

A rare complication of Crohn's disease is primary sclerosing cholangitis (PSC), which Paul developed in his mid-thirties. PSC is a chronic disorder that leads to inflammation of bile ducts in the liver. The ducts serve as the liver's plumbing system and allow bile to drain. When this system doesn't work, scarring occurs, leading to cirrhosis and liver failure,[2] which Paul also developed.

PSC symptoms include itching, fatigue, yellowing of the skin or whites of the eyes, and infections. PSC progresses slowly but inexorably; no treatment has been shown to cure or slow its progress. Instead, treatment aims to relieve symptoms and manage complications. Liver transplantation is the only remedy for liver failure.[3] Ten years of aggressive PSC management delayed Paul's need for a transplant, but ultimately, it was his only recourse.

During the process of being listed for the liver transplant, a colonoscopy revealed precancerous lesions in Paul's large intestine. A family history of colon cancer, combined with disappointing colonoscopy results, necessitated a total colectomy (removal of the large intestine) before he could be listed.

God must have a sense of humor because I was placed on the transplant list on April Fool's Day. After only twenty-four days, I gratefully received the liver of a young man who died much too soon. It was April 1996, and I was thirty-nine. I often think of that man's family and the sacrifice they made. Their decision gave me life, and the antirejection drug Cyclosporine prevented organ rejection.

By the grace of God, I came through this experience with flying colors. The surgery took only four hours, and I required no blood transfusions—a rarity. I went home from the hospital in four days and was back at work within four weeks.

The liver transplant happened long before Paul and I met. Unfortunately, we both endured dismal first marriages for over twenty years. "Dismal" seems like a short word to describe those years, but it works perfectly.

Both of our spouses left for someone else. We were betrayed by untruthful and unfaithful mates. If I hadn't lived it, I couldn't have comprehended the despair of living through such miserable circumstances. Every day was heartache; it was a difficult season of life. Our spouses abandoned us, but in so doing, they freed us to start over. It's an amazing thing to receive a second chance, and we don't take it for granted. Not even for a day. I'll tell you more about that later.

Back to November 2011. The morning after Paul's seemingly innocent sip of Diet Coke was his scheduled liver biopsy at Houston's St. Luke's Episcopal Hospital (SLEH) in the Texas Medical Center. Although we live in northwest Houston, an hour from the hospital, we prefer the medical center over outlying facilities because of Paul's extensive medical issues and need for top-notch specialists.

Dedicated to "the glory of God and the service of mankind," SLEH opened in 1945. Early milestones were the first successful heart transplantation and the first artificial heart implantation. Associated with Baylor College of Medicine, St. Luke's Kidney Transplant Program is dedicated to providing the highest level of patient care, and more than 1,500 kidney transplants have been performed there since 1986. [4]

FIRST MATCH

Before telling you more about our journey through Paul's medical issues and how his sip of Diet Coke changed our lives, I have to tell you about our other story—the story of how we met, fell in love, and forged a new life together not so long ago.

I was single for four years before I met Paul; he was on his own for a year. He shared Thanksgiving 1999 with my sister, Cynthia DeLaughter, and her husband, Dennis, as well as Dennis's brother Roger DeLaughter and his wife, Lorinda. Cynthia and Roger saw a potential match between us and suggested that Paul give me a call. He must have looked miserable, and Cynthia knew I was.

Paul gathered up enough courage to call a few weeks later—at 10:15 p.m.! He was in the midst of Christmas choir rehearsals and decided to call me when he got home one evening. Little did he know that I got up for work every morning at 4:30 a.m. and was sound asleep when he called.

I had no idea who this man was or why he would call at such a late hour until he said the magic words: "Cynthia told me to call." Ohhhh. That made him okay. Of course, Cynthia had neglected to mention him to me.

We talked for a while until he finally asked if I wanted to go out. It had been twenty-five years since I had dated and wasn't at all sure I knew what to do on one. Paul didn't act like he knew too much about it either. By this time, I was in serious jeopardy of falling asleep, but accepted his invitation anyway. He sounded like a nice person, and if Cynthia liked him, he must be all right, so why not? Little did I know that I would fall head over heels, madly in love shortly after meeting him.

Our first date—a blind date in the truest sense of the word—was to a church Christmas concert in Katy, Texas. It wasn't love at first sight, but it was close. We arrived late.

During the week leading up to our date, I waited for Paul to call and ask for directions to my house, which happened to be an hour and a half away from his house. He never did. I was certain that he didn't know exactly where I lived. I was in the rural community of East Bernard; he was in northwest Houston.

By the afternoon of our first date, I started to suspect that he expected me to *meet him* at the church. At this point, let me insert that I'm what you might call old school. It never occurred to me to meet him there. I knew that picking me up would involve a lot of driving back and forth, but he *was* the guy.

Standing in our kitchen, my seventeen-year-old daughter Cindy and I talked about it. She suggested that he probably meant for me to meet him so that I'd have my own car and could leave whenever I wanted. It was as if we were meeting at a bar, and I might need to drive myself home if he got drunk! She said that's what people did nowadays on first dates.

I didn't think that was a good idea. I knew we weren't going to be drinking, and that I could trust Paul since Cynthia had vouched for him. He was crazy if he thought I was going to drive myself to our first date!

A few minutes later, he called. By this time it was almost 6:00 p.m. The concert started at 7:00 p.m. It would take him an hour and a half to get to East Bernard and another forty-five minutes to get us back to Katy. The clock was ticking.

In his roundabout way, he sort of suggested that I meet him. In my more direct way, I suggested he come pick me up. He mentioned that we would be really late to the concert if he came to East Bernard. I agreed. We *were* going to be late, and he should hurry if we were to make it to any of the concert. He came to East Bernard.

And that's why we were late. Nevertheless, we had a good time and went out for dessert afterwards. Thus began our courtship.

We were both fragile. Inexperienced. Scared. We had been through a lot with spouses who had used and abused us. In our mid-forties, we were no longer young and naive. To imagine that there was actually someone out there who could be trusted with love was almost unthinkable.

But we started dating anyway, and he always came to pick me up. E-mail was an integral part of our budding relationship. We wrote back and forth at least once a day, sometimes more often. I saved them all. Honesty became our mantra. When you've lived with lies for so long, truth is critical, and we settled for nothing less.

Not long afterward, Paul asked me what I was looking for in a husband; I smarted off that I wasn't looking! That was only partially true. Although I didn't think such a person existed, I had made a mental list. My mythical husband had to

- know what to do when I cried,
- love God,
- know how to sing,
- be financially stable,
- make me laugh, and
- love me more than he loved himself.

This was quite a list, which was why I didn't think anyone could satisfy it, and why I wasn't looking. There were reasons for each item on the list. I wasn't going to settle for anything less than what I knew was right for me.

Amazingly, Paul met all my criteria and many more. We went from strangers to soul mates within six months. Some of his e-mails illustrate the progression of our relationship after our first date that December:

> December: *"I really enjoy your company and spending time together."*
>
> Early January: *"I thank God each day for allowing you to come into my life. Whenever I check my e-mail, it seems like forever until it tells me if there is a message. Then I just wait on pins and needles to find out if it is from you. See what you've done to me!"*

It was exactly the same for me. I could hardly wait to hear from him every day!

> Mid-January: *"It was so good to hear your voice tonight. I could listen to it forever. I hear a tenderness that melts my heart. Was it always there or have we grown much closer in the past week or so? Either way, I love to hear your voice. You are my undoing. I can't stop thinking about you. Sharon, you have become part of me. I don't understand how it happened in such a short time.*

About a week later, God spoke to me. If you haven't heard that small voice in your head, this may sound suspect. But God really does direct our lives, and if we listen, his voice can be heard. I had learned to pay attention to that voice but was unprepared for what he said.

Out of the blue and without a doubt, God told me that Paul was "the one." He was the man I should marry. To say that I was surprised would be a serious understatement. I was surprised that God revealed it and even more surprised that there was someone who met my criteria!

I hardly knew Paul. We had only been out a few times, and we hadn't even kissed! Nevertheless, I heard that voice all day, reassuring me that Paul was indeed the man I was to marry. He was "the one." This had a profound effect on me, and I was very grateful. Without this confirmation, I don't know if I would have entertained the thought of marriage. I had already made one mistake, with awful consequences. I wasn't up for another one.

God also gave me a profound love for Paul that day. I can't explain it; all I know is that when I woke up that morning, we were dating. A few hours later, he was my beloved. I couldn't live without him.

Gathering my courage, I called Paul and confessed my love. I didn't tell him that he was "the one." I needed him to figure out if he loved me on his own, not marry me because of some God-mandate! He e-mailed shortly afterwards:

> *"I am so in awe that you love me! You have made me the happiest man in the world! I have read Ephesians 5 all my life and have known what it says about a husband loving his wife as Christ loved the church and gave himself for it. This is the first time I've understood it in my heart as well as my head. You have brought me joy and freedom; you have sent me to another planet!"*

> Late January: *"You are everything I think of. You are heaven-sent; you are love; you are passion; you are in my every thought; you are my desire; you are my answer to prayer; you are my vision of a godly woman; you are a super mom; you are my support; you are my completion;*

you are the air I breathe; you are my everything. Sharon, you are my true love."

February: *"I don't know what I ever did without you. You must be from heaven, for God has perfected his plan for my life by bringing you into mine."*

God's confirmation, as well as our love for each other, gave me confidence to pursue a relationship with someone who carried a lot of medical baggage. But I was scared. Paul's medical problems were a serious consideration. I had no desire to be the caregiver to a sick husband. Although I'm a nurse, and I love being a nurse, I didn't want to be one at home. Neither did I want to get married only to become a widow. I couldn't see the future and was afraid to risk loving then losing.

But God knew what I needed. We were a perfect match. When Paul proposed marriage, I said yes. Yes to Paul. Yes to love. God offered a second chance, and I gratefully seized it, deciding that it would be better to love Paul for six months than to never love at all. I have never, not for one moment, regretted it.

After a whirlwind courtship, we married in June 2000— six months after our first date. It was a simple but incredibly meaningful ceremony. My brother Milton Anderson performed the ceremony and my sister Cynthia was matron of honor. Paul's brother David Ragsdale was best man.

Paul was blessed with a beautiful baritone voice and sang Neil Diamond's "The Story of My Life" at our wedding.

This was a surprise; he didn't understand the concept of the bride being in charge of the wedding! I had planned for my brother-in-law Dennis to sing another song. But Paul decided differently and sang these sweet words:

> The story of my life begins and ends with you…
>
> I was alone but you found me waiting and made me your own.
>
> You're the story of my life, and every word is true;
>
> Each chapter sings your name, each page begins with you.
>
> The story of my life is very plain to read.
>
> It starts the day you came and ends the day you leave.[5]

I didn't cry on our wedding day, even while Paul sang, although nearly everyone else did. I wasn't nervous, and I didn't second-guess my decision. There was perfect peace that all was well, and that I would never regret marrying Paul. Time would bear this out, but it was nice to know ahead of time.

Between us, we had four children: Jason, Kristen, Cindy, and Lindsay. At the time of our wedding, their ages ranged from fifteen to twenty-one years old. Jason and Kristen were already living independently; Cindy and Lindsay were at home. None were overly thrilled about us getting married, but they gradually came to understand that we were better together than apart.

Following God's plan wasn't always easy. For the first year of our marriage, we lived in two different cities, sixty miles apart. Cindy was a high school senior in East Bernard; Lindsay was a high school freshman in Cypress. We didn't want to disrupt either daughter, so we spent the weekdays in our respective cities and weekends at one house or another. We could have waited to marry until Cindy graduated, but decided against it.

I had no intention of waiting a year to get married. God had given his blessing, and I had waited my whole life for a love like Paul's. We set the soonest date possible!

This arrangement meant that we had two yards to mow, two houses to clean, two sets of utility bills, etc. Although difficult at times, it was the best thing for the girls. God gave us strength to weather the storm, and Sharon moved to Houston as soon as the school year was finished.

We each disposed of about half of our furniture so that everything would fit in one small house. It was so good to be together under the same roof, it didn't matter what we had to do to make it work. This experience forever cured us of wanting a vacation home. One house was enough. With Sharon's touch, my depressing house became our beautiful home. My sister Julia said, "Your house looks like it came out of a magazine." Sharon's transformation of our home was nothing short of remarkable.

Moving to Houston was tough. I left everything—job, family, home, friends, and church. Except for college, I had lived my whole life in a rural area. I was accustomed to visiting with friends in the grocery store and knowing everyone at church. In contrast, I knew only one person in northwest Houston—Paul. But I went willingly and wholeheartedly. My life was imbedded in Paul's heart, and I didn't care where we lived.

The next eleven years were medically stable ones, except for a three-week hospitalization in 2007. Paul managed a solid equilibrium between health and illness and enjoyed a normal work, church, and social life.

The years were full of good times as well as trying times. We celebrated our children's graduations and marriages. We also walked through the terror of drug addiction and divorces. Our three grandchildren—Victoria, Justice, and Jake—are amazing. And we have been blessed to be part of Metropolitan Baptist Church and then Houston's First Baptist Church.

In 2009, we felt God's leading to open an eleven-bed, residential, assisted-living home. This was a huge leap of faith. Neither of us had ever owned a business, and we were accustomed to regular paychecks!

Paul, who had become a real estate broker, found a great house in an established, wooded neighborhood that suited our purposes. We continued to look for a year, but the first house we saw turned out to be the best. We spent seven months updating the house so that it met all Texas Department of Aging and Disability Services regulations as well as our own design preferences.

We had four aging parents, so all decisions were based on whether they would hypothetically be happy living there. It was to be a living space but also our workplace. Between the regulations, family concerns, and my personal aesthetics, there were many structural and design changes.

Cypress Assisted Living, LLC was the result. Seven bedrooms accommodated eleven senior adults—all ladies except my dad. Licensed in 2010, we opened our doors and entered the world of elder care. We have been blessed with residents ranging in age from 65 to 104 and have loved them all.

I had planned to continue working in medical sales for another year, but it didn't turn out that way. My position was suddenly eliminated, and I found myself out of work. The worst thing about this development was that it took away our medical insurance.

As you might guess, Paul is uninsurable. Since realtors don't have insurance benefits and I had lost mine, he was forced to use the state pool insurance, which commands a very high premium. The state accepts those who cannot receive coverage from any other company. We kept our COBRA insurance for the maximum eighteen months and then went to the state pool. There was no other choice.

THE BLESSING

Sharon has a special gift of "hearing" from the Lord. I have often wished that God would place a neon sign in front of me so I could know his will. That hasn't happened, but I have learned to never get in the way of what God tells Sharon. It is a wonderful opportunity to hear his voice, and I am truly thankful for it.

I can count on one hand, with a couple of fingers left over, how many people I've told about "the blessing." I've held it close to my heart for over ten years because it was so personal, so precious, that I dared not breathe it aloud. I don't deserve it, and surely didn't earn it, but like God's grace, it was given anyway.

During a church worship service in 2001, God whispered four words: "I will bless you." I had heard God's voice before, giving direction for major and minor decisions. He had never lied to me or led me astray. His words had always proven true and had taken me down the right path.

So when I heard these words, it gave me pause. It was easy to trust him, and I knew at once that he would indeed bless me. I didn't know how, but I knew he would. As time passed, I occasionally wondered about the promise that I labeled "the blessing."

I had ideas. My most heartfelt desire was that all four of our children, their spouses, and our grandchildren, would know Jesus as their Savior and grow spiritually. I wondered if God would bless us financially. After a while, I decided that whatever God's plan was, it would be good, and there was little hope of guessing the future. I kept "the blessing" in the back recesses of my mind and almost forgot about it.

On a Thursday in May 2007, a dear friend of ours, Karen, died after a long bout with colon cancer. She was forty-seven. I was struck with an overwhelming sadness at her loss. Her young adult children, still trying to find their way in the world, desperately needed her. She would never know her grandchildren. Life would never be the same for her husband. I cried relentlessly.

The next day, in the midst of my grief, God spoke these words of comfort, "This is what I spared you." I would understand this more fully in December of that year then again in November 2011. But the message was clear enough—God was going to preserve Paul's life. I praised him through the tears and wondered what the future would hold.

On Saturday, the day of Karen's funeral, God spoke again. I guess he thought I could put two and two together and then realized I couldn't because he said, "I told you I would bless you." The light bulb flipped on as waves of understanding flowed. If not for "the blessing," Paul would have died at forty-seven, like Karen.

A 2003 liver biopsy, performed when Paul was forty-six, had revealed recurrent primary sclerosing cholangitis (PSC), the original disease. We were stunned at this diagnosis, completely unaware of the rare possibility of its return in the transplanted liver. There was preliminary discussion of the need for *another* liver transplant. However, five subsequent biopsies over the ensuing years revealed *no* PSC. With each one, Dr. Risë Stribling, Paul's hepatologist, explained that the negative result simply meant there was no PSC in the specific spot that was biopsied. Nevertheless, Paul was already fifty. He had been spared once with the original liver transplant and again at forty-seven.

One of my darkest days was when Dr. Stribling reported that the PSC had returned. My sadness was overwhelming, but somehow I knew God would not leave me, and that he had a purpose for my life.

I realized it was okay, even as a Christian, to be depressed. It is only a season. Our true joy comes from a personal relationship with Jesus Christ that does not depend on circumstances. I cannot fathom facing the storms of life without Christ faithfully carrying me.

Fast forward to 2007 when Paul experienced repeated bile duct infections. The infections were a result of bile duct blockage within the liver. The connection, or anastomosis, between the liver and the small intestine had narrowed, and liver sludge accumulated because it couldn't drain. This was a big problem.

We didn't know that sludge was a medical term, but it turns out that it is. Bile sludge is a mixture of substances that precipitate from bile. Bile is the fluid that is made by the liver and stored in the gallbladder. After eating, it travels from the gallbladder, through the common bile duct, and into the intestine to help digest fat. If the bile duct doesn't drain properly, sludge accumulates and becomes a source of infection.[6]

Since the anastomosis had narrowed, the only thing that kept Paul's main bile duct open was an external biliary tube, which radiologists threaded into the liver to allow bile to drain into a bag outside his body. The tube was replaced every three to four months under anesthesia and kept viable for four years. But they constantly clogged, causing infections, which resulted in scarring.

The transplanted liver was at risk, which was another big problem. Although the surgeons didn't want to reoperate, it was deemed necessary. A hepaticojejunostomy revision was performed by Drs. John Goss and Christine O'Mahoney at St. Luke's Episcopal Hospital on December 3, 2007.

Hepaticojejunostomy is a big word that meant the surgeon cut the bile duct where the new liver was attached, trimmed off the damaged end, and sewed it back together. The liver docs had been telling me for years that we needed to do it, but they felt it was too high risk. After four years of biliary tubes, which no longer prevented infections, all options had been exhausted. That surgery was my only choice.

Previous abdominal surgeries had caused internal scar tissue, so surgeons warned that the procedure was going to be difficult and time-consuming. Generally, the more surgeries a person undergoes, the more scar tissue accumulates. Cutting through and around this fibrous tissue can be both challenging and dangerous; surgeons treat these traumatized abdomens with great respect. While cutting through scar tissue, other structures can be inadvertently sliced, leading to bleeding and other complications. Nevertheless, surgery was unavoidable.

We were understandably nervous, but friends and family gathered to pray, and peace prevailed. As it turned out, there was amazingly little scar tissue, and instead of a two-hour procedure, they finished in forty-five minutes! For a couple of days, Paul's recovery seemed to be on course.

That changed when days became weeks and his small intestine never "woke up." He was diagnosed with bowel obstruction although the cause was undetermined. For twenty-one days, Paul could neither eat nor drink. Not even a sip of water was allowed, unless he wanted to vomit it back up. Nothing was going through that blockage.

There were some long, despairing days while surgeons debated the solution. Multiple abdominal scans and x-rays uncovered no source of obstruction. Paul was hungry, thirsty, depressed, uncomfortable, and cranky! It was during this time that the brotherhood of Christian men ministered and comforted him. One afternoon in particular, he hit an all-time low, and I couldn't think of anything that would help.

I stepped out of the hospital room that he had been in for almost a month and called several of his friends, asking them to come when possible. Of course, they were at work, but Courtney Cravin, a friend from Metropolitan Baptist Church, dropped everything and drove across town. Paul's brother David also came. Their visits helped him turn the corner.

None of the surgeons—and I mean not one of them—wanted to reopen a fresh incision. Newly developing scar tissue made the abdomen very vulnerable during this time. They wanted the body to repair itself, as it often did in these cases. But eventually, Dr. Randolph Bailey, who had performed Paul's original colectomy in 1995, was consulted to investigate the obstruction.

One of the initial partners of Houston's Colon and Rectal Clinic, Dr. Bailey is nationally recognized for the quality of his patient care and the expertise he demonstrates as a leader in colorectal disease treatment. We were thrilled to have him on Paul's case.

I told Dr. Bailey, "Most surgeons don't get to go back and take a look at their work fifteen years later!" This was my fourth major abdominal procedure—two liver surgeries and two colon surgeries. My abdomen looked like a road map with scars going in all directions.

Of course, the only way Dr. Bailey could "take a look" would be to take Paul back to surgery, which is exactly what he did.

Before going back to the operating room, a group of family and friends prayed for me. Dennis, my brother-in-law, acknowledged that God was in control and that we would bow to his plan. It was true.

Dr. Bailey discovered that a loop of intestine had fallen through a triangle of intestinal loops. He performed an enteral hernia reduction and tightened up that triangle so it wouldn't happen again. Paul's recovery was on track from then on, and he was home by Christmas.

This was all part of "the blessing," and more would come.

PART TWO:
SHUTDOWN

NEEDING A NEW KIDNEY

After enjoying relatively good health for several years, a new bombshell was dropped in August 2011 when physicians said I needed a kidney transplant. At a routine liver appointment, one of the hepatologists said in passing, "Oh, by the way, you know you're going to need a new kidney pretty soon." Uh, no, we didn't know that. By the next appointment, it was, "I guess we need to start the kidney workup. Are you on dialysis yet?" Again, that would be a no.

We weren't completely ignorant. Paul had struggled with renal insufficiency for years due to a complication from the immunosuppressant drug Cyclosporine. Developed twenty years previously, it was the drug of choice to prevent liver transplant rejection and had saved countless lives. Unfortunately, a long-term side effect was kidney failure,[7] which was Paul's situation.

Although we knew about the renal insufficiency, we really thought he was okay. We were wrong. We had not understood the significance of long-term renal insufficiency.

I keep a spreadsheet of all lab values dating back to 2000. Looking at the steady rise in creatinine levels, I was shocked. The physicians had been keeping an eagle eye on the creatinine for years, but we hadn't understood how important it was. It had gone from a relatively normal 1.5 in 2008 to 3.65 in 2011. That was a big problem.

Creatinine levels reflect kidney function. It increases as the kidneys' ability to filter fluid within the body decreases. A creatinine result over 1.4 mg/dl may be an early sign of declining kidney function.[8]

Glomerular filtration rate (GFR) is another strong diagnostic indicator and decreases with kidney failure. The GFR is the rate that blood is filtered through the kidneys and is normally over 90 mL/min/1.73m^2. A GFR below 60 is a sign that the kidneys are not functioning properly; a GFR below 15 indicates kidney failure, and that dialysis or a transplant will eventually be needed.[9]

Paul's GFR had gone from 45 in 2008 to 18 in 2011. We were stunned when we realized the significance of that 18. Together, the creatinine and GFR levels revealed that Paul was on the verge of serious kidney failure.

Upon realizing this, our goal was to have a kidney transplant *before* Paul required dialysis. Research has shown that transplanted kidneys last longer and function better if they are grafted in before dialysis.[10] This was important. If he was going to need a transplant, we wanted it to have the best possible chance of survival. Paul's daughters Kristen and Lindsay, his sister Julia, friend Susie Pipkin, and I were ready to be tested for donor compatibility. Each of these potential donors was healthy and had acceptable blood types. Their offers were genuinely viable and we were extremely grateful. If I wasn't compatible, we would have to accept one of these offers.

Paul and I did everything we could to facilitate a transplant before dialysis was initiated. We met with kidney and liver specialists, talked to two different organ donation programs, visited with multiple insurance representatives, and generally made a pest of ourselves to everyone potentially involved. It was not to be.

Before Paul could be cleared for a kidney transplant, his liver had to be given a clean bill of health. That was the reason a liver biopsy was scheduled in November, coincidentally on the morning after the coughing was triggered by the Diet Coke incident.

We had planned to spend the first week of November in Las Vegas with my sister Cynthia and her husband Dennis. Months of planning had gone into the trip, and we were all looking forward to getting away. But since we were still trying to facilitate a pre-dialysis transplant, the liver biopsy took precedence over a vacation, so we cancelled the trip. I am absolutely convinced that if we had been in Las Vegas during the coming crisis, Paul would not have survived.

LIVER BIOPSY

On November 2, 2011, we checked into the hospital for Paul's liver biopsy. Impaired kidney function had caused him to have decreased clotting capability. For that reason, the biopsy was to be performed through the jugular vein instead of a direct puncture to the abdomen, a procedure he had undergone many times.

This worried us. Anytime you say the word "jugular," terrifying thoughts of uncontrollable bleeding come to mind. I hadn't forgotten about a previous abdominal liver biopsy that had hemorrhaged and required a blood transfusion of four units.

However, they assured us that the jugular was the safer route, so we agreed. As it turned out, the biopsy was uneventful, and subsequent results showed the liver was doing well. This was a *huge* relief because of the 2003 biopsy showing a recurrence of primary sclerosing cholangitis, which would have necessitated another liver transplant. It would certainly have precluded the current kidney transplant.

On the flip side, Paul continued to cough after the biopsy. Remember the coughing? I was the only one concerned about the blasted coughing! I kept telling the physicians about the Diet Coke the previous night, but they discounted it completely. It was frustrating because it seemed important. It had obviously triggered *something*, and that something wasn't good.

Paul had started spitting up blood that morning, and it gradually increased in volume. By early afternoon, almost every cough produced bloody sputum. His lungs were congested, and he was having trouble breathing unless he sat up. Even so, they were ready to send him home by 2:30 p.m. The biopsy was over, and discharge papers were written.

That didn't seem right. Call me crazy, but coughing plus blood plus lung congestion plus immunosuppression plus respiratory distress plus recent invasive procedure equal *a problem.*

Enter our nurse friend, Joy Lasco, who worked in interventional radiology, where the procedure had taken place. Originally, the liver biopsy was to be performed by one of the physician fellows, a doctor training in that specialty. Joy had already checked on Paul and was instrumental in honoring our request that Dr. Barry Toombs, a senior radiologist we knew from past experience, do the procedure.

I asked Joy to question Dr. Toombs about the coughing and respiratory distress. He checked on Paul again, ordered a chest x-ray, and called Dr. Stribling, Paul's hepatologist. She "suggested" that he be admitted to the hospital for overnight observation. Fully expecting Paul's resistance, Dr.

Stribling relayed this message, "Don't make me come over there!" This proved to be our only laugh of the day.

I met Dr. Stribling more than ten years ago when she came to Baylor College of Medicine from UCLA. When she entered the room during my first appointment, I thought, What can this young woman know? She looks like she's barely out of medical school! *But over the years, we developed a warm friendship; I trust her implicitly. She has conscientiously protected my health, and I think she hung the moon in the liver world.*

Paul was *intensely* disappointed about the hospital admission. A deer hunting trip with close friends was approaching in two days. A year of planning, research, conversation, and anticipation had gone into that trip. The overnight hospital stay put the trip in jeopardy, and he knew it. I, however, was acutely relieved. The progression of the cough into continuous bloody sputum, and now, respiratory distress, was very troubling.

I sometimes wish I could just be "normal," whatever that is. The physical limitations that have plagued me for my entire adult life can be overwhelming. I am usually able to "go with the flow," but sometimes, unexpected complications throw me. This was one of those times.

We moved from interventional radiology to a holding room on the sixth floor where patients wait before undergoing outpatient procedures. Because Paul was a transplant recipient, hospital stays were always on the twelfth floor, which was typically full. Since transplant patients are immunosuppressed, this unit is equipped with special air-filtration systems that help prevent infections. We waited for four hours while the bloody coughing continued and his breathing worsened. Getting oxygen into his lungs was becoming increasingly difficult.

The nurses on this unit were accustomed to healthy preoperative patients with few complications. Paul didn't fit that mold. I became progressively worried and believed it absolutely crucial that we get to the twelfth floor. But all transplant floor beds were full, and he could go nowhere else. My efforts to facilitate a move were met with resistance and lackadaisical attitudes. The biggest problem was that no one recognized Paul's escalating shortness of breath. In truth, I didn't realize the seriousness of the situation either, but I knew we needed help.

By 7:00 p.m., our nurse told us we had a room, but now we had to wait on transportation. Transportation is the department that moves patients from one location in the hospital to another. These are always nice people who work very hard. Of course, they are not at the patient's beck and call. They are sent out as requests are received although there are certain patients who receive higher priority, such as those who are seriously ill.

It was also shift change, which made matters worse. Having worked in hospitals for many years, I understood shift change; it's a hectic time. But we had a problem that superseded shift-changing issues. We waited until 7:45 p.m. with no move in sight. Desperate, I decided to take matters into my own hands, found a wheelchair down the hall, and brought it to our room so that I could take Paul upstairs. We could wait no longer.

Sam, our nursing assistant, intercepted me and said that I could not move Paul. Although he was bigger than me, I told Sam that I could, and would, if he didn't. He decided he could, and we arrived on the twelfth floor with only moments to spare.

CRISIS

Shortly after Paul was settled into bed, he was in serious trouble. Our nurse, Kham Thai, was an ICU nurse who was floated to the twelfth floor that night. He assessed Paul and quickly called hospitalist Dr. Victor Narcisse, his admitting physician. Even though he was sitting straight up, Paul was unable to breathe and was coughing up blood with every ragged breath. He couldn't get enough oxygen.

I now realized that Paul was in a life-and-death struggle, and he was losing. Kham was in the process of initiating aggressive treatment and trying to get Paul transferred to the ICU, but it wasn't happening fast enough.

All of a sudden, Paul decided that he had to go to the bathroom! He wanted to walk to the bathroom. For the record, I'm usually in favor of going to the bathroom when you need to go. However, this was not a good time. Let me repeat, this was not a good time. He was moments away from complete respiratory failure, and going to the bathroom was not the priority. Paul, on the other hand, was adamant.

I suddenly realized that he was confused due to oxygen deprivation. That was when I started worrying about whether he would survive the night. Kham, Dr. Narcisse, and I were in absolute agreement that he remain in bed. I looked him in the eyes and told him, "Stay. In. Bed. Please." He did.

Kham had mobilized a respiratory therapist to the room as well as other nurses. Dr. Narcisse asked me to step outside. I had to leave the room. I had to leave Paul. This was the most difficult thing I'd ever had to do. I had to trust someone else to do what I couldn't. Kham and the others needed space to work, and I was in the way. I stepped out.

Dr. Narcisse called a code. Code Blue is broadcasted throughout the hospital when a patient has stopped breathing or has no pulse or is in imminent danger. A red cart is rushed into the patient's room, and preassigned medical professionals rush from all over the hospital. For some reason, I didn't hear it over the PA system, but I saw the cart.

Instead of feeling panic, I was intensely relieved. We were finally getting what we needed. Inside that cart were the tools of life, and with it came a pulmonologist, critical care nurses, and the intensive care unit (ICU).

Out in the hall, Dr. Narcisse apologized for calling the code before Paul actually stopped breathing. He didn't want to scare me but was having trouble getting everyone he needed to the floor. I told him, "No problem, do whatever you have to do to save Paul's life. I'll agree to anything. I'll sign anything."

My one request was to not use "practice people." No practice people. Gripping his jacket, I looked him straight in the eyes and said over and over, "No practice people. No practice people." He finally said, "Okay, no practice people." He got it.

Like other medical center hospitals, St. Luke's is a teaching facility. There are always "practice people" on the critical care teams—residents, fellows, and nurses who have minimal resuscitation experience. They have to get practice somewhere, on someone. But not now, not tonight. Paul had come too far to gamble with the inexperience of "practice people".

While the code team was busy, I stood alone out in the hall. I was scared *out of my mind*, more frightened than I've ever been in my life. Paul's life was hanging by a thread, a very slim thread. I went to the end of the hall and started praying, "Jesus, help us…Jesus, help us," over and over. It's the only thing I could think of.

The nursing supervisor asked if I had any family. Well, of course, I had family. By this time it was well after 10:00 p.m., and they were at home, asleep! She knew that Paul was spiraling down fast. He was later diagnosed with simultaneous kidney, heart, and lung failure—a triad of events that many patients do not survive.

Having my family sounded like a great idea, but I knew what I really needed was Jesus. We needed divine intervention in the worst way. We needed God to show up, and we needed him *right now*.

I frantically called my sister Cynthia and asked her to rush to the hospital; then I called our daughter Cindy a few minutes later. She reported that Cynthia was still getting dressed, so they hadn't left yet. (Cindy, then twenty-nine, and her husband, Rett, were living with Cynthia for a couple of months while they bought a house.) I distinctly remember saying, "Hurry up, or Paul will be dead by the time you get here!" After hanging up, I thought, *Oh dear, that didn't sound good, but it was the brutal truth.*

The evening was unequivocally the worst of my life. Nothing had prepared me for this. Too scared to cry, I had never experienced anything that even approached the horror of losing Paul. I knew very well what life without him was like. I'd suffered through twenty-two years in an unhappy marriage and four years as a single mother. To lose the love of my life after only eleven years was heartbreaking.

Our first date was the beginning of joy. Marriage had generated love, happiness, and true freedom. After these few years of bliss, I was watching it go down in flames. It rocked me to the core.

I remember not being able to breathe. No matter how deep or how often I took a breath, I couldn't get enough oxygen. I saw the crash cart come into the room and thought, I'm in real trouble. *And then,* I hope they can just give me some oxygen. *I would not realize the desperation of the moment until God's hand was so obviously revealed after the crisis passed. I remember the Ambu bag coming toward me and those first few breaths being the sweetest I'd ever taken. Dr. Narcisse ordered them to push the intravenous drug Versed, and everything went peacefully black. The next four days didn't exist.*

Inside the hospital room, Paul was being sedated, intubated, and oxygenated. If you haven't been oxygen-deprived, there is no way to understand how it feels. Paul learned the hard way.

It was like diving deep in the ocean and trying to swim my way to the top for air. Then just as I approached the surface, someone raised it another twenty feet! Over and over I struggled. I didn't know what had happened but knew I would die from lack of oxygen if someone didn't intervene.

The trip to the seventh floor Cooley cardiovascular ICU was a blur. There wasn't enough room in the elevator for me since the respiratory therapist was bagging Paul, and Dr. Narcisse, pulmonologist Dr. Alberto Colomer, Kham, and others accompanied him.

I argued for about two seconds, realized it was a losing battle, and gave up. Only those essential to Paul's survival were getting on that elevator, and I wasn't one of them. When the elevator doors closed, I didn't know if I'd see him again alive. Another nurse told me to follow him; he knew a shortcut that would allow us to intercept the group before they made it to Cooley.

Dr. Narcisse went out of town the following week but said that God kept bringing Paul's case to his mind. When he returned, he told us what had really happened in the elevator. As the doors shut, he realized that the treatment wasn't working; Paul's oxygen saturation was deteriorating instead of improving. He had run out of options and was losing Paul. That's when Dr. Narcisse started praying…and that's when God saved Paul's life. God showed up in the elevator. And he showed up just in time.

By the time they arrived on the seventh floor, oxygen saturation had improved, and Dr. Narcisse knew that it wasn't because of what he and Dr. Colomer had done. The nurse who ran the shortcut with me was right; I met up with Paul for just a few sweet seconds before he was rolled into the ICU.

I didn't know about what had happened in the elevator, but Paul was alive, and God was in control. I was still scared out of my mind but tremendously relieved to have made it to the ICU.

MIRACLE AFTER MIRACLE

Once Paul was stabilized, Dr. Colomer did a bronchoscopy and lung "washout." Still sedated, a bronchoscope was inserted down Paul's throat. Lighted and equipped with a small camera, the bronchoscope allowed visualization of the airways and pinpointed the source of bleeding and subsequent respiratory failure.

Paul was experiencing alveolar hemorrhage—an uncommon, acute, life-threatening condition in which blood floods the alveoli. Alveoli are the millions of tiny sacs where the oxygen and carbon dioxide transfer takes place in the lungs. Survival depends on that transfer. Treatment consists of high doses of intravenous steroids and antibiotics, mechanical ventilation, supplemental oxygen, and bronchodilators.[11]

Normal lungs appear dark on an x-ray because they contain mostly air, which allow x-rays to easily pass through. If fluid accumulates in the lungs, fewer x-rays will make it through to the film, and those areas appear white. The white areas are called infiltrates, which represent a variety of problems, among them infection, pulmonary edema, or hemorrhage.[12] In Paul's case, it was the latter.

Dr. Colomer asked if I wanted the details or just an overview. I wanted everything. He took a deep breath and explained that the next twelve hours were critical. If the progression of infiltrates didn't turn around soon, it probably never would. Those were hard words to hear.

Accessing the computerized series of chest x-rays from the last twelve hours, Dr. Colomer described them. At 2:30 p.m. (after the liver biopsy), there were minimal but definite white areas on the right lower lobe of Paul's lungs. By 8:30 p.m., about 75 percent of *both* lungs were scattered with infiltrates. By 9:30 p.m., it had escalated to 90 percent, and both lungs were almost fully white. This was when Paul went into respiratory failure on the twelfth floor. It was a rapid and astonishing deterioration.

I had not yet been allowed to go into Paul's ICU room but could peek through a small window. Sedated, intubated, and on the ventilator, he was resting.

I began to consider the miracles that had happened so far.

- Dr. Tombs reevaluated Paul before discharging him.
- Instead of going home at 2:30 p.m., Paul was admitted.
- The hunting trip was cancelled.
- The Las Vegas trip was cancelled.
- We had an ICU nurse on the twelfth floor who initiated aggressive treatment.

- Dr. Narcisse called the code before Paul actually stopped breathing.
- God showed up in the elevator.

The miracles were accumulating...

STUNNED

Throughout the crisis, there was an intense inner nervous energy that I could not quiet. I couldn't bring myself to sit, and I was constantly hopping up and down. I felt like a bunny rabbit on steroids. I knew I was hopping up and down and tried to stand still, even sit, but couldn't.

I was still scared crazy, but I also felt a peace deep within. Many prayers were being offered up on our behalf, and I could feel God's power at work. I am absolutely convinced that these initial prayers, and those that would continue for the next several weeks, were our lifeline to survival and sanity.

By midnight, family and friends had responded to my calls and arrived at the hospital. I ran/hopped back and forth between the ICU hallway and the waiting room, as much to give myself something to do as to update them.

After Paul was stabilized, it was time to wait for the treatment to work. The ventilator did all the effort of breathing. Multiple intravenous lines administered antibiotics, steroids, and fluids. A Foley catheter drained urine. Other lines monitored vital signs and blood oxygen saturation. Nurses, physicians, and respiratory therapists went in and out, but Paul was thoroughly sedated.

As with most ICUs, there was a rule that prevented family members from staying overnight in the patient's room. I understood the need for this rule but simply had to remain nearby. I would have slept out in the waiting room but greatly preferred to stay in the room.

I heard Dr. Narcisse tell the admitting nurse that he'd rarely seen a family member stick up for a patient like I had, and that they might consider letting me stay close. Because of his suggestion, the nurses let me remain in Paul's room. I actually wasn't aware of the overnight rule until a week later.

There are no sleeping chairs in ICU. One chair offered a slight recline, so it and another chair for propping up my feet became my bed. I was grateful and slept like a rock for a couple of hours.

God's mercy prevailed, and his healing hand sustained Paul through the night. After a couple of hours, the infiltrate was slightly less dense and started to clear a tiny bit at the top of both lungs. *This was very good news.* He had a long way to go, but he survived the immediate crisis, and much more treatment would follow.

An echocardiogram done the next day estimated that Paul's heart function had dropped from a September ejection fraction (EF) of 45 percent to 20–24 percent. Normal is 55–70 percent.

During each heartbeat cycle, the heart contracts and relaxes. With contraction, the heart ejects blood from the ventricles. When the heart relaxes, the ventricles refill with blood. No matter how forceful the contraction, the ventricle is never completely emptied. The term "ejection fraction" is the percentage of blood that's pumped out of a filled ventricle with each heartbeat.

In other words, ejection fraction is very important. Paul's had plummeted. An EF of less than 40 percent can be indicative of heart failure. An EF of less than 35 percent is diagnostic of life-threatening irregularity,[13] especially in the presence of fluid overload.

Paul's ejection fraction of 20–24 percent was completely unexpected. Cardiologist Dr. Sayed Feghali explained that the heart had been "stunned,"[14] and he expected its previous function to return within a few days or months, if it was going to return. I wanted to know if he was *certain* it would improve or if he just *hoped* it would. Of course, there was no guarantee. He replied that if he didn't expect improvement, he wouldn't do any more echocardiograms!

That gave me a tiny measure of hope, but the fact was that this change in cardiac status instantly meant that a kidney transplant was impossible; I dreaded having to disclose this to Paul. Dr. Feghali's minimum EF requirement for surgery was 45 percent, and Paul was nowhere close to it.

This was a heartbreaking blow with catastrophic long-term implications, including lifetime dialysis and a significantly shortened lifespan. It didn't seem possible, much less fair. After everything we'd been through, this was what it came to. I moved forward out of sheer will and faith. There were few options.

Because of the decreased EF, the blood backup had caused congestive heart failure, enlarged the heart's left ventricle, and engorged the lungs. The kidneys had failed, which contributed to systemic fluid overload. Paul had a lot of problems.

The medical team agreed that initiating dialysis was imperative. This would relieve the overload and allow Paul to wean off the ventilator, which was the immediate goal. Every day spent intubated increased the complication rate.

A central line in the jugular vein was inserted by Dr. Christine O'Mahony for the first dialysis. A surgical resident had been scheduled to perform this procedure, but I insisted on Dr. O'Mahony once I knew she was available. I knew and trusted her. Again, no practice people.

The nurse tried to intimidate me by saying that this could delay dialysis, which would not be in Paul's best interest. I wholeheartedly agreed, so I suggested they get Dr. O'Mahony as soon as possible. Thankfully, she was able to come right away, and I was very grateful.

During those first critical ICU days, one of the residents at our facility, Cypress Assisted Living (CAL), passed away. It was not unexpected; she was currently on hospice, but it was a big deal. Although our elders are advanced in age, we're rarely ready to let go. Each one is an integral part of our community. Their families are our family, and we take every loss personally. I always want to be there.

Unfortunately, this was not a good time to leave Paul. It was, in fact, impossible to leave. I was forced to leave the situation at CAL in the capable hands of the hospice nurse and our staff. They were amazing, as usual. I stayed at the hospital and grieved with the family from afar.

WAKING UP

Paul had been sedated for three days since his crash on the twelfth floor. Due to potential hepatic toxicity, the liver team discontinued one of the drugs that was keeping him sedated. As a result, he began to wake up enough to start pulling on tubes.

There were a lot of tubes: a central line in his neck, an endotracheal tube down his throat, a nasogastric tube in his nose, four intravenous lines in his arms, a urinary catheter, circulation pumps on both legs to prevent blood clots, an oxygen saturation monitor, a blood pressure cuff, and many heart monitor pads scattered across his upper body. Each line was critical because it either relayed information or provided lifesaving treatment.

While I was out of the room during one of the mandatory 6:00–8:00 p.m. visitation breaks, restraints were applied to both of Paul's arms. When I returned and discovered them, I was appalled. Restraints are a huge issue and are used in hospitals to restrict a patient's freedom of movement.

There are three types of restraints: physical (manual force), mechanical (straps), and pharmacological (drugs).

The only two circumstances in which a hospital can rightfully employ restraints are when

1. a treatment plan that includes restraints has been agreed upon by staff and patient/guardian.
2. staff determines that the patient will be harmed unless he is restrained and there are no other options.[15]

Paul did not fit into either of these categories, and I was furious that he had been tied down. Although it was true that he could have harmed himself by inadvertently pulling out the endotracheal tube, I had not agreed to a treatment plan that included restraints and a very viable option was that I could be there to help prevent their extraction.

If a patient is not *completely* sedated, being restrained is torturous. If you are doubtful, try tying both arms to a chair for fifteen minutes. Or an hour. Then try it for four hours. It is unacceptable unless absolutely necessary.

I swallowed my anger and asked the nurse if I could remove the restraints as long as I was at the bedside and could keep him from pulling out tubes. She reluctantly agreed and kept a close eye on us. I repeatedly told Paul that if he didn't want to be restrained, he'd have to remember not to pull the tubes. This was difficult since he was still partially sedated, but he learned quickly and was compliant. The restraints were not reapplied.

It was during this time that he was able to communicate through writing. His first words were heart-wrenching.

"Where am I?" I couldn't believe I hadn't thought to tell him. I cried for the first time.

"Did I almost die?" to which I had to answer yes.

"Breathing was so hard, I thought I was going to die." I know.

Later that day, *"Are we still at SLEH* (St. Luke's Episcopal Hospital)*?"* Yes.

"I need music." I brought in a CD player.

"God is so good." Yes, he is.

"Thanks for being here. It means a lot." Where else would I be?

"Don't go out in the hall." One of the doctors had suggested we talk in the hall. Paul signaled no; he wanted us to stay in the room. He was afraid they were going to tell me he was dying, and I wouldn't tell him. We stayed in the room, and I told him everything.

"I love you." I love you too.

"What is today?" He had missed a few.

"Are routine finger sticks necessary?" Because of the massive steroid dosing, his blood sugar was sky-high, and yes, the every four-hour sticks were necessary.

"Confused." Although dialysis was starting to clean out the toxins, it was slow going, and he became confused—a terrifying experience.

"Can you stay tonight?" Yes.

"Did you call my folks? Kristen? Lindsay?" Yes, yes, and yes. *"I've never had a bed bath."* Today will be your first.

Pulmonologists were concerned about complications. Although ventilators are lifesavers, physicians prefer to wean patients as soon as medically feasible. Ventilator-associated pneumonia is a frequent and life-threatening complication with mortality rates of 33–50 percent.[16]

By late afternoon, Paul was awake enough to start coming off the ventilator. The weaning process progressed quickly, and the endotracheal tube was pulled. It was replaced with a full face mask for high-flow oxygenation. There are a variety of oxygen delivery systems. Room air contains only 21 percent oxygen; oxygen delivered through a nasal cannula increases the concentration to just 30–35 percent. A tight-fitting face mask (or non-rebreather mask) results in up to 60–80 percent oxygen concentration.[17]

I vaguely remember my brother-in-law Dennis and daughter Lindsay visiting soon after being extubated. Nervous about getting enough oxygen and dying before I had told my daughters one more time about how important Jesus is to me, I started crying. The only thing on my mind was that I wanted my girls to know the peace Christ brings.

I had no idea why Paul was crying, but it added stress to an already difficult situation. It's hard to breathe and cry at the same time when your lungs are full of blood! After asking Dennis and Lindsay to step out, we talked privately. When he told me about wanting to tell the girls about Jesus again, I assured him that he had already done that, many times.

I went out in the hall and asked Lindsay point-blank, "Do you remember your dad talking to you about Jesus?" She exclaimed, "Yes! Of course!" So I asked her to go back and reassure him that she knew about Jesus, which is exactly what she did.

Paul soon tolerated ice chips, so the nasogastric tube was removed. This was wonderful progress! Although exhausted from the effort, he ate some Jell-O. I was thrilled that he was doing so well.

With such rapid improvement, I decided to go home for the night. I had been at the hospital around the clock for three days and was ready for a shower. This turned out to be premature.

I slept like a rock until Paul called at 5:00 a.m. the next day, frantic and struggling to breathe. I had left the cell phone under his pillow, which turned out to be a wise decision. Gasping, he explained that he couldn't get his nurse to understand that he was in respiratory distress. He wasn't getting enough oxygen with the new mask. She insisted that all was well, but it wasn't.

We disconnected, and I immediately called the ICU nurses' station, asked for the charge nurse, and told her what was happening. She called the pulmonologist, ordered a chest x-ray, and asked the respiratory therapist to reevaluate Paul's oxygen status.

The x-ray verified that there was still significant lung consolidation, so more aggressive oxygenation was instituted. Nobody wanted to reinsert the endotracheal tube, least of all Paul, but the struggle to breathe had become a superhuman effort. If it didn't ease up, he'd have to go back on the ventilator.

I got back to the hospital by 6:00 a.m., guilt-ridden that I hadn't been there when he needed me. He had struggled most of the night, continuing to cough up blood and having to sit straight up to breathe. The pulmonologist admitted later that he probably should have waited another day to pull the endotracheal tube and apologized. The higher-flow oxygen and mask change helped considerably, and he was able to stay off the ventilator.

This experience reinforced Paul's newly acquired fear of not being able to breathe. It was terrifying, something that cannot be imagined until experienced. Several more days of adequate oxygenation had to pass before he was able to conquer the panic.

I held on to that oxygen mask for dear life, like a toddler holds on to his security blanket. Every time I moved from my bed to a gurney, the nurse would say, "Just slide over first and then we'll put the mask back on." They didn't realize the panic of being without oxygen for even a few seconds. I didn't care what they did or where they took me as long as the oxygen came with me.

Dialysis continued every day for a week, with an eventual fluid loss of forty-five pounds. It was essential that the overload be relieved, and in fact, the goal was to induce mild dehydration.

Bruce Plummer, close friend and American-Indian pastor in Montana, had a three-hour layover while passing through Houston. Our friend Tim Black found out about it and fast-tracked him back and forth to the hospital so he could pray with Paul.

Waking up to see Bruce's strong prayer warrior's face was such a blessing, and the fact that he happened to be in Houston was testimony to God's grace. Bruce is a dear friend, and I will always remember his special trip to pray for my recovery.

TO SING OR NOT TO SING

Paul has been singing for God's glory since he was a teenager, and he has a wonderfully mellow baritone voice. John Bolin, Minister of Worship and Arts and gifted songwriter at Houston's First Baptist Church, had written a song with Paul's voice in mind for the 2011 *Celebration*.

This annual Christmas event features a three-hundred-member choir, full orchestra, and many volunteers. Secular and sacred Christmas songs tell the story of Jesus, climaxing with his death and resurrection. In 2011, six performances would be enjoyed by eighteen thousand people in the greater Houston area.

"At Last" was a trio featuring a king, shepherd, and Simeon—all of whom awaited the Messiah's arrival. Paul was honored and humbled with the opportunity to sing the king's part and had been growing a beard for the occasion. By November, that beard was full—which was great for the performance but uncomfortable and awkward with the oxygen mask in place. Singing a taxing *Celebration* solo was now out of the question.

While in the ICU, I asked the cardiologist if he thought I would be able to sing. He replied, "I'm not going to say it's

impossible, but I am going to tell you it is almost impossible."
Since I could barely whisper, much less breathe and sing at the
same time, I had to agree.

Paul texted John, suggesting that he find a replacement;
singing in a few weeks would require another miracle. A
big one. When John came to visit soon afterwards, he told
me privately that the song was Paul's and that he wasn't
giving up. I had huge doubts and, frankly, just wanted him
to survive. But the song was important to Paul, and John
knew it.

Paul came to a spiritual decision during the night.
He surrendered the song. An unfamiliar flaw—pride—
had crept in, and he wanted no part of it. He told me to
bring his shaver to the hospital so he could shave off the
beard, and that's exactly what he did. It was an act of total
spiritual obedience.

If God wanted him to sing on December 8, he'd have
to restore Paul's voice, his body, his stamina, and his breath
control. He wouldn't discredit the song by singing with
only half a voice.

Tim Black came by to offer some much needed
encouragement. He and Paul had forged a strong bond
during a Montana Indian mission trip four months earlier.
Paul could barely speak but wanted to say something. He
lifted the mask away from his face so that he was still
getting oxygen and with a pitiful, raspy voice, said, "God's
ways are not our ways."

He lay back and replaced the mask. I worried when he exerted himself on nonessential communication, but I was clearly "not the boss of him," as he loves to say. At least not at the moment. A minute or so later, he repeated, "God's ways are not our ways." Then a little later, the same thing, "God's ways are not our ways."[18] Tim and I were choked up by now, knowing this was important. Paul had learned it the hard way.

The mission trip with Tim had been a busy time, and we did many things for the Lord. But after this crisis, it occurred to me that in the beautiful Montana mountains, I had been so intent on "doing" that I had missed the glory and beauty of God's creation. I regretted that. God used this situation as a reminder that God's glory is everywhere, and we should pay attention to what he really wants from us. My mind still goes back to the Montana mountains when I hear the song "Don't Let Me Miss the Glory."[19]

MANAGING THE FLOW

Three days after Paul began dialysis, the jugular line was not allowing adequate blood flow, so a large intravenous catheter was inserted in Paul's femoral vein. Because the catheter increased the risk of blood clots and infection, he was on strict bed rest, but it provided great dialysis access.

A central line is not a regular intravenous catheter. It is a long, flexible tube used to deliver medication, fluids, nutrients, or blood products over an extended time. Inserted into a large vein, it is eased in until it reaches a large vein near the heart.[20] In Paul's case, it made dialysis possible.

Because of the increased risk for infection, I constantly worried about the central lines. He had been on immunosuppressant medications for sixteen years and was much more likely to contract an infection than the average person. But there was simply no other choice, and we prayed harder for protection.

The 100 percent high-flow oxygen continued and Paul's breathing eased. Nevertheless, I had to put up a No Visitors sign and enforce it strictly. The problem was that whenever a visitor came, Paul felt the need to be "okay." Although talking was exhausting, he kept on until he was panting from the effort.

Truthfully, it was also difficult for me. I appreciated the company, but in order to maintain stability, I had established a strict daily routine. Breakfast in the basement cafeteria was at 6:00 a.m., when all ICU visitors were asked to leave for two hours. Lunch depended on what was happening with Paul. Supper was at 6:00 p.m., again when we were asked to step out. Bedtime was after midnight, when it quieted down. Deviating from this schedule was difficult; the fewer decisions I had to make, the easier it was to manage.

Visitors had to be updated, assured of progress, and apologized to for Paul not being able to interact. Others in the room meant that I had to leave because of the two-person limit. This left Paul "in charge" of company and his own minute-by-minute care—an impossible task for an acutely ill patient. For all these reasons, and although their motives were the purest of the pure, visitors had to be strictly limited for Paul's health and my sanity.

At the same time, there was a *constant* flow of physicians, residents, physician assistants, nurses, respiratory therapists, nursing assistants, x-ray technicians, dieticians, social workers, housekeepers, and case managers. The only quiet time was between midnight and 4:00 a.m., when lights were dimmed and noise kept to a minimum. Except for two trips home, I slept at Paul's bedside every night for the first week. It comforted both of us.

LONG NIGHTS

By November 7, five days after the initial crisis, Paul had made significant improvement. He was eating regular food and even had a little energy. Nights were easier, without the shortness of breath. However, daily dialysis completely zapped his strength. To Dr. Feghali's surprise, the ejection fraction had not improved. We were completely disheartened.

A tunneled catheter was inserted in Paul's upper chest, providing more permanent dialysis access so that the femoral catheter could be removed. Discontinuation of the femoral line meant that he was able to get out of bed and sit in a chair. This catheter would be his dialysis access for the next five months.

For five to six days, I was on strict bed rest. While sedated, it was no problem. But after waking up, I was miserable. I wanted to get up so badly! I kept looking at the floor, thinking, It's only three feet to the floor, but it might as well be a mile. *I just wanted to jump up and walk. When I was finally given permission to get out of bed, I tried to "jump up" and only managed about a half inch. What little muscle I had entering the hospital was gone, and I had to relearn how to walk.*

Elevated lab results and dialysis inflicted havoc on Paul's mental orientation during this time. Blood urea nitrogen (BUN) is a blood test that reveals how well the kidneys and liver are working. High levels are indicative of poor kidney function. Normal is 8–24 mg/dl;[21] Paul's was sky-high at 116.

To make matters worse, nephrologists explained that brain chemistry is often altered during dialysis and results in confusion, nightmares, and changes in the perception of time, place, and person. Paul was not spared this phenomenon. He struggled to explain what was going on in his mind but really couldn't. This was one of the most difficult things of the entire experience for him; his worst nightmares were on November 7.

That was the longest night of my life. Dialysis and elevated lab values were causing horrific nightmares; I can't describe how frightening they were. I saw images of friends and family being brutally torn apart in death. The final blow came when I dreamed Sharon was killed along with all the others. I awoke many times during the night, staring at the clock on the wall; even the clock deceived me—the time always appeared the same. I was in total agony. My entire life was ruined because all the people I loved were dead. Time stood still.

In the ICU room, a curtain hid the chair where Sharon slept. I tried to look over and see if she was really gone but couldn't see her. Finally, I realized that God would never do this to one of his children, so it must be a lie. I recited over and over, "I will never leave you or forsake you,"[22] knowing God would keep me strong. I never doubted his Word, and am so thankful that when bad things happen, God is still there. The next morning, I found out it was the first day of daylight savings time, and we had lost an hour. In addition, the clock in my room needed a new battery, so time really had stood still.

At 4:00 a.m., I heard Paul banging on the side rails. I jumped out of my chair and went to his side. Sobbing, he told me about the nightmares. After realizing I was truly alive, he said over and over, "You're here…you're here." We cried together, and I was so grateful that I *was* there.

After this incident, Paul needed to be able to listen to the Bible. I called our friend Tim, who promptly arrived with a NowBible. It was an electronic device that narrated the full text of the Bible through earphones. Paul kept it on his pillow and listened to God's Word day and night. It was a huge comfort. He was declaring that "his mercies are new every morning"[23] when he woke up the next day.

Nursing staff gradually made it clear that I could no longer stay overnight in Paul's room. The hour-long drive back and forth to our house was a problem since it prevented me from getting back to the hospital quickly. The recent nighttime crises made me very reluctant to leave the immediate area. I needed a new strategy.

I searched throughout the hospital and found a flat, upholstered bench in the basement conference area, which I dragged into a nearby ladies' restroom. Along with a chair, it provided a place to stretch out and rest undisturbed. The restroom lights could even be turned off, which was a real bonus. This plan worked perfectly, and I slept for five hours. By 4:30 a.m., I was awake and back in Paul's room.

My efforts to remain nearby for so long may seem strange, but for me, it was vital. Paul and I had been to hell and back, and I couldn't watch from afar as he struggled. He would have done no less for me.

Wedding Day: June 24, 2000

Paul and Sharon, after 2007 hospitalization

Paul and Sharon, 2008

Atop the Empire State Building

2009

Paul always looks great in a tux! Christmas 2010

Sharon

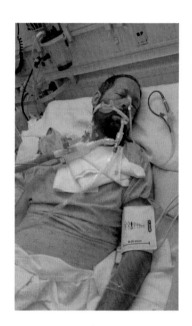

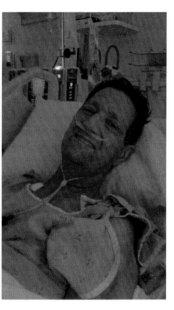

Paul in ICU: 11-3-11

A few days later, without the beard, and off the ventilator

Graduation Processional: Those honor
cords were the result of a 4.0 GPA!

Graduation: Cindy, Rachel, Cynthia, Sharon, Paul, Faye, Jason

Miracle Man in King's costume at Celebration
2011: Lindsay, Victoria, Paul, Kristen, Justice

Christmas 2011: Paul, Sharon, Jake, Rett, Cindy,
Victoria, Lindsay, Jason W., Kristen, Jason J., Justice

Grandchildren Justice, Jake, and Victoria, 2011

To God be the Glory!

paul and sharon

Paul is still wearing the defibrillator
(see black strap). We didn't get this 2011 Christmas
card out until January, but we just had to celebrate!

Ringing the Transplant Bell

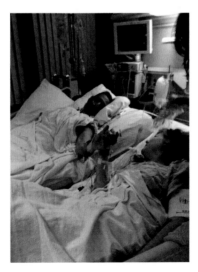

Five hours post-op in ICU, 3-30-12

The picture of health, May 2012

Celebration 2012

Hunting with Rett

Never a dull moment!

JESUS LOVES US, THIS WE KNOW

The next day, November 9, Paul was weaned off 100 percent high-flow oxygen and placed on wall oxygen. This was a big milestone and meant he could soon leave the ICU. However, as his respiratory status improved, dialysis and cardiac complications continued.

As I gained strength and was able to take a few steps in my room, I wanted to roam around. At one point, I took a few steps out in the hall toward the nurses' station. You've never seen nurses move so fast! They weren't used to their patients walking around!

Paroxysmal supraventricular tachycardia is a condition that involves an occasional rapid heart rate, ranging from 150–250 beats per minute.[24] The stress of dialysis triggered Paul's heart rate to jump to 180–190 beats per minute on two occasions. Since the normal rate is 80–100 beats per minute, and he was in heart failure, ICU staff took this very seriously. There was little wiggle room for complications.

Paul knew immediately when his heart started fluttering and learned to zone out to a peaceful place in his mind. This helped him relax and allow the medication to work.

When my heart rate spiked, I tried to concentrate on calming thoughts to help bring it back down. The first time this happened, Sharon had gone home for some well-deserved sleep. About 5:00 a.m., I felt my heart rate jump sky-high. If a normal heart rate feels like walking, tachycardia feels like running superfast.

I didn't want to alarm Sharon, so I just rode out the storm and didn't call her. They administered medication that decreased my heart rate, which took a few minutes, but worked. After the medication had taken effect, it felt like my heart was a herd of wild horses trying to gallop, but someone was holding the reins tight. It took about an hour and a half for the pseudo-galloping to go away.

After Sharon arrived, I didn't mention it. Then it happened again. She strongly *encouraged the nurse and me to never leave her out of the loop again. She had left strict instructions with both of us to call her if there were any problems. Since I knew that I would have felt the same way if the situation were reversed, I decided not to do that again.*

When the tachycardia reoccurred, the red cart was brought back in the room. This was the same type of red cart that had helped resuscitate Paul a week earlier. I cringed while the ICU code team hovered over Paul with defibrillator paddles in hand. It scared the daylights out of me. IV medication restored a normal heart rhythm within minutes, but it felt like hours.

One of the things that helped calm my heart rate was to stare at the ceiling and mentally sing "Great Is Thy Faithfulness."[25]

I sang that song over and over in my head. Once again, God's peace prevailed. The song helped me, but not Sharon. It was strange to look over at nurses holding paddles, ready to deliver a shock. I knew I wasn't in control, but God was. In the really desperate times, I was able to draw on memorized scripture or songs, which served as my foundation in a crisis.

Toward the end of every dialysis treatment, Paul's blood pressure would plummet to approximately 50/30. Normal is 120/80. The dialysis nurse would replenish fluids to his system, which helped stabilize the pressure. Then he'd stand up, and it would drop again. This prevented any hope of ambulation or physical therapy for days.

While still in the ICU, with all the machines and tubes, I called Sharon to my bedside. I told her that "we have to praise God even now, not because we like what's going on, but because he tells us to." So we did. We found that praising him made the good times better and the bad times tolerable.

I decided to go home that night. I needed to check on our assisted living residents as well as get some uninterrupted rest. It made me *really* nervous to be so far away from the hospital, but I was hoping that the crises had passed.

I cried most of the drive home, worried about Paul's cardiovascular issues. He seemed so fragile, and there were so many opportunities for disaster. I was unaccustomed to the three new organ failures—kidney, heart, and lung. Managing liver and GI issues had kept us busy for years but in no way compared to the current situation. Although aware of his renal insufficiency, we were blissfully ignorant of what it might eventually involve. Now, no longer.

I wanted to be everything God wanted me to be; I wanted to trust him no matter what happened. But the truth of it was that my horrible, gut-wrenching fear was that if I gave up control, God would take Paul home. To heaven. Away from me.

It all came crashing down on me that night. The terrible certainty was that I was not in charge, and I could not make him better. I simply did not have it in me. The physicians were doing their best, but they were also limited and had admitted as much on more than one occasion.

It then occurred to me that "there is no fear in love."[26] If that was true (it had to be) and if God loved us (I knew he did), and if he is faithful (yes, he is), then I shouldn't be afraid. I had to trust someone, and God was the best I had. In all my years with him, he had never disappointed or deserted me.

So this was my prayer as I drove home: "I know you love us. I know you are faithful. I know you are trustworthy. Whatever your plan, I accept it. My prayer is for Paul's health to be restored and to come home. But I refuse to be afraid." Peace washed over me with sweet relief, and I slept all night.

SCHOOL

No medical crisis comes at a good time, but this happened to be a particularly bad time. Three years earlier, I had gone back to school to earn a Master of Science degree in nursing education at Texas Woman's University (TWU). It had been an interesting, albeit humbling, journey that Paul had encouraged every step of the way. He endured much moaning and groaning that stemmed from my ineptitude and insecurities. It had been thirty-two years since graduating from TWU's College of Nursing, and to say that I was a computer novice was an understatement.

Each class was a challenge. Every research paper was difficult. My constant thought was that as soon as the professors realized how little I knew, they'd toss me out of the program, and all my work would be for naught. Those three years of graduate school had stretched me about as far as I could be stretched. I knew that God had led me in this direction, but my most secret fear was that he was preparing me for a life without Paul. Somehow, he was going to use this new degree to help me support myself when push came to shove. I couldn't decide if this was a good plan or a horrible one.

However, I had to trust that his plans for me were good, because he is good. All that is to say, my educational thesis was due to be defended before a committee of TWU professors the very week that Paul hovered between life and death.

In addition, my computer crashed, and I crashed right along with it. The paper needed final editing. I could no more decide which computer to buy, download all the programs, and then restore the old data than I could fly to the moon. Without a plane. Those were things that Paul would have done, but not at the moment.

My brother-in-law Dennis graciously helped determine which laptop to purchase and spent hours restoring software and files. Before the computer glitch, I couldn't figure out which to be more worried about—Paul or the paper. I had worked on it for eight months and was set to graduate if I could successfully defend by the deadline. Of course, I had been worrying more about Paul, but the paper was on my mind too. I prayed for God to help me finish the paper and for his mercy to fall on those professors; I needed school to be over.

In the meantime, Paul insisted on praising God for everything. Even in his bleakest moments, he declared that we had to praise him in the good times and the bad. I had to agree; however, I was thinking that this would probably qualify as the bad. But if Paul could, I could. He was the one lying in the ICU trying to work up enough strength to walk.

Every day was a blessing, and we were learning to give God our deepest fears, so thankful for his faithfulness. The physicians were continually amazed at Paul's progress, in several instances giving God the glory and personally praying for Paul. It was a comfort to know that they leaned on God. We told each of them that everything they did was covered in prayer. We particularly told this to the surgeons since they held the scalpels.

On November 15, I walked in the rain from the hospital to TWU for my paper defense. It was only a couple of blocks from St. Luke's, but it seemed a long way. They were long blocks, and I didn't have an umbrella! It had been a busy day in Paul's room, but I'd had plenty of time to get nervous, and now I was soaking wet.

Upon arrival, I saw that my primary instructor was on the phone; the other was also busy. This caused a delay in our meeting, and I was irritated. I thought, *Here I've spent two semesters working on this project, bought a new computer, walked over in the rain, have a husband in ICU, and I'm the only one on time. You guys are sitting in your offices talking on the phone without a care in the world. The least you can do is be on time!* I felt plenty sorry for myself.

Then I realized that this was a God-given opportunity to relax, gather my thoughts, and pray. Goodness knows I needed it. I was suddenly very grateful for the break, and by the time they were ready, I was ready. Three undergraduate nursing students happened to be in the room and were invited to listen to my presentation. That suited me just fine since they served as a buffer between me and the professors.

Everyone was gracious and offered suggestions for further editing. Most importantly, the professors signed off on my December graduation. Those signatures meant that I was, for all practical purposes, done.

I walked down those TWU steps feeling lighter than a feather. In another month, I would actually go to Denton, attend the commencement ceremony, and graduate with a Master of Science in nursing.

But for today, I was done.

GOING HOME

On November 18, after sixteen days in the ICU, Paul was moved back to the transplant floor. His lungs continued to clear, he was walking the halls, and his mind was sharp. The four-hour daily dialysis sessions had been decreased to every other day. On the flip side, heart function remained at 20–24 percent, and two units of blood were given due to low hemoglobin.

We struggled with the long-term implications of this "new normal" and continued to ask our prayer warriors for intercession before the Lord. All our prayer requests made me feel very high maintenance. Literally, hundreds of people were calling out to God on our behalf. I was very aware that each of them had their own problems, schedules, and lives. We were deeply aware of God-given strength because of their faithfulness to pray. We are wholly in their debt.

The cardiologist insisted on doing a heart catheterization to rule out blockage. Thankfully, it revealed no obstruction, and Dr. Feghali was confident that Paul's heart function would improve, although he was mildly surprised that it hadn't already. In the meantime, Paul was required to wear an external defibrillator since his ejection fraction remained at 20–24 percent.

The defibrillator was a vest designed for patients at risk for sudden cardiac arrest and was removed only for bathing. It continuously monitored Paul's heart and would deliver a shock treatment, restoring the heart to normal rhythm, if he went into life-threatening arrhythmia.[27]

Although this was meant as a safeguard to prevent catastrophe, it scared us silly. Paul alternated batteries every twenty-four hours, but the defibrillator sometimes alarmed anyway. If one of the straps turned over and all the sensors weren't fully touching his skin, it alarmed. If the charging unit malfunctioned, it alarmed. If Paul shifted his position a certain way, it alarmed. If he forgot to switch the battery, it alarmed.

At first, we thought he would be shocked every time the alarm sounded, but we soon learned that only an emergent arrhythmia would cause a jolt. In that case, we wanted it, but it was scary. It was a constant reminder of his heart's fragility, and he wore it night and day for two and a half months.

Physicians have a language all their own. An example is the word "sick." For instance, if "Joe" has pneumonia, the physician will report to the family that Joe has pneumonia; he will be treated with a course of antibiotics and inhalation therapy. There is a definite course of action, and Joe is expected to recuperate.

However, if the infection fails to respond to antibiotics and respiratory failure ensues, the physician will comment that Joe is "sick." If he doesn't improve and cardiac complications arise, Joe will be "very sick." The physician may not be specific, but this is an attempt to warn family members that Joe doesn't just have an illness; he may be knocking on death's door. Loudly.

The family assumes that Joe has been sick since he started coughing. Not so. He became "sick" when he developed complications; he became "very sick" when those complications became life threatening.

Throughout Paul's November hospitalization, *every* physician offered the same report: "Your husband is *very* sick." I knew exactly what they were saying. Every declaration humbled me because I knew they cared and were doing everything in their power to facilitate his recovery.

Paul has had some of the most gifted physicians and surgeons in the country. One of the infectious disease specialists, Dr. Kevin Grimes, noted that Paul's list of doctors read like a *Who's Who* list of liver, kidney, heart, lung, and colon experts. Without their diligent care and expertise, this book would not have a happy ending. But as much as they helped, it was God who brought healing.

Paul was discharged on November 19, extremely thankful to be home. I was thankful that I wasn't coming home alone. I had gone through this entire experience with no mouth ulcers, which is how my body usually reacts to stress. Although insignificant compared to Paul's medical problems, ulcers were painful, took weeks to resolve, and made eating uncomfortable. Unbelievably, I hadn't had even one. Numerous people had been praying, and this was confirmation of God's protection over me as well as Paul.

Many friends and family members had come to our aid. Without them, we would have faltered, and our business would have suffered. There was a tender ministry of the brotherhood of Christ. To a person, their mantra was, "We'll do anything, anytime." Our daughter Cindy and friend Tim Black were close by and constantly "on call."

A passage in 2 Corinthians affirms how God, along with family and friends, "rescued" us from despair:

> We don't want you in the dark, friends, about how hard it was when all this came down on us in Asia province. It was so bad we didn't think we were going to make it. We felt like we'd been sent to death row, that it was all over for us. As it turned out, it was the best thing that could have happened. Instead of trusting in our own strength or wits to get out of it, we were forced to trust God totally—not a bad idea since he's the God who raises the dead! And he did it, rescued us from certain doom. And he'll do it again, rescuing us as many times as we need rescuing.
>
> You and your prayers are part of the rescue operation—I don't want you in the dark about that either. I can see your faces even now, lifted in praise

for God's deliverance of us, a rescue in which your prayers played such a crucial part.

Now that the worst is over, we're pleased we can report that we've come out of this with conscience and faith intact, and can face the world—and even more importantly, face you with our heads held high. But it wasn't by any fancy footwork on our part. It was God who kept us focused on him, uncompromised."[28]

KIDNEY DONORS NEEDED

Twenty-six million Americans suffer from chronic kidney disease while four hundred thousand are on dialysis.[29] Heart disease is the major cause of death.[30] If you don't have a family member who is included in those numbers, you may have quickly skimmed over the last two sentences. But if someone you love is on dialysis, please read on, carefully.

Diabetic nephropathy is a kidney disease that affects diabetics. Each kidney is made of hundreds of thousands of tiny nephrons, which filter blood and help remove wastes from the body. Nephrons in diabetics thicken and gradually become scarred, which causes protein to leak into the urine.

Kidney damage often progresses for up to ten years before symptoms are noticed. Treatment goals focus on preventing disease acceleration. One of the best ways to accomplish that goal is to keep blood pressure below 130/80. Once large amounts of protein appear in the urine, kidney damage will slowly worsen and lead to the need for dialysis or transplant.[31]

Despite its vulnerability, the kidney has an enviable position when it comes to transplantation. Since most people have two, a donor can part with one and live a completely normal life. If, however, you are among the group of people—the odds are 1 in 750—who are born with only one kidney,[32] you should keep it! Most of these people are unaware that they have only one kidney.

Although living kidney donation is a viable option for many, it has not gained the acceptance it deserves. As of April 2013, there were 96,103 Americans on the kidney transplant list. Fewer than 17,000 receive a kidney in any given year. In 2012, there were only 5,619 living kidney donations. Unbelievably, that number is shrinking.[33]

Instead, deceased donors account for the bulk of kidney transplants, 10,868 in 2012. If you are willing to consider this option, notify key family members. You *truly* will not need your organs after you die. Others will.

These numbers represent real people. Individuals are dying, and families are losing precious loved ones. Insurance isn't the problem since kidney transplants are federally funded through Medicare. Clinical expertise isn't an issue since medical technology is highly advanced and offers donors low-risk surgery. The truth is that renal failure patients are dying because of the simple lack of volunteer donors.

Many dialysis patients are reluctant to ask family and friends to test for donor compatibility. Sometimes a volunteer steps forward, but the patient declines. Individuals are willing to continue dialysis, not fully understanding the havoc it wreaks on their bodies. It will eventually be obvious, but by then it may be too late for transplant.

BORROWED TIME: LIFE ON DIALYSIS

Dialysis is another world. Everyone is on borrowed time, and they know it. Paul seemed among the healthiest while some arrived by ambulance.

Dialysis is the artificial means of doing what healthy kidneys do—getting rid of waste and water in the blood. Normal kidneys also regulate mineral levels and produce erythropoietin and calcitriol as part of the endocrine system. However, dialysis can't correct these issues; it only takes care of waste and fluid removal. In the end, dialysis is only a stopgap measure until the patient receives a transplant or dies from kidney failure or associated complications.

About 1,500 liters (or 396 gallons) of blood are filtered by a functioning kidney each day. In the absence of a functioning kidney or dialysis, waste products increase and eventually reach levels that cause coma and death.

A regular intravenous site isn't large enough to accommodate the large amounts of blood that are pumped in and out. A surgical procedure enlarges a blood vessel to accommodate a dialysis catheter. During hemodialysis, the patient's blood circulates through a large machine that has special filters.

The filters do what the kidneys normally do then return filtered blood to the patient.[34] The patient is connected to the dialysis machine until enough fluid and waste has been removed for the patient to live another few days. It's a never-ending process, and nothing supersedes dialysis. It becomes the number one priority.

At least it did for us. Dialysis took precedence over all other scheduling. Other physician appointments were worked around it. All business and social events took a backseat. We saw other patients miss dialysis and assumed they must be in the hospital or had met with other dire circumstances. Paul never missed an appointment.

Outpatient dialysis was scheduled for every Monday, Wednesday, and Friday. Each session required the same four hours that it had in the hospital. Fortunately, we were accepted into a hemodialysis center only a few miles from home. At first, Paul was too weak to drive himself but, by the third appointment, was able to manage it.

The dialysis center physicians and nurses kept pushing me to get a fistula, which requires a surgical procedure where an artery and vein are connected for dialysis access. If I had a fistula, the tunnel catheter could be removed, which would reduce the risk of infection. Every time they asked when I was going to have the surgery, I told them I didn't need it; I was going to have a transplant. They were awed since few had that opportunity, but I had a peace that God would provide a kidney.

The duration of each dialysis depends on how well the patient's kidneys work and how much fluid weight has been gained between treatments. Dialysis patients are on a strict dietary regimen. Excess protein, potassium, sodium, phosphorous, and fluid are extremely harmful since dialysis cannot do what a normal kidney does.

Foods that should be strictly avoided are frozen and canned foods, fast foods, milk, cheese, soft drinks, ice cream, potatoes, chocolate, nuts, whole grain bread, cereal, cake, fish, poultry, bacon, sausage, hot dogs, lunch meat, dried beans, brown rice, peanut butter, raisins, fresh fruit, yogurt, tomatoes, and salt substitutes.[35] Paul loved all these except tomatoes; for the first time in his life, he had a valid excuse to avoid them!

Hospital dietary instruction consisted of a dialysis nurse's nutrition chart outlining what Paul should and shouldn't eat. Dialysis websites provided vital instruction until the first outpatient dialysis appointment, at which time we received extensive dietary counseling.

Fortunately, Sharon is very research-oriented, and we didn't suffer from lack of information. She printed off pages and pages of dialysis nutritional requirements, which really helped. By the time we met with the dialysis dietician, we knew some questions to ask.

Paul was strongly advised to drink less than 1½ liters per day, or 48 ounces. That may sound sufficient, but it really isn't. I bought a 48-ounce pitcher that we filled with water every morning. When it was empty, Paul drank nothing else. He soon learned to pace himself so that he had some left for nighttime. After a couple of weeks, he knew exactly how much water he could drink without the pitcher.

The fluid restriction was by far the most difficult aspect of the dialysis regimen. His body was in a constant state of dehydration, which is exactly what physicians wanted. We quickly learned what he could and could not eat, but the limited fluids were the real challenge.

The hardest part was in the beginning when I would sit down for breakfast and know I could only have a few sips instead of really drinking. I looked at the little water pitcher that Sharon filled each day and knew that was all I could have for the next twenty-four hours. I just wanted to take big gulps of water, but couldn't.

Throughout the day, I chewed on ice. Never enough, it was the only option. Part of the "fluid budget" was what I needed for my meds. I was taking over thirty-five pills a day and needed a few sips morning and night to get them down. Every swallow counted. (Do the math; I had taken over 210,000 pills since the liver transplant sixteen years earlier.)

While I downed full glasses of tea and Diet Coke, Paul could only have sips. I felt more than a little guilty about it. Thankfully, he took complete charge of the renal diet and fluid restriction. It would have been impossible for me to enforce. Other families struggle. After a while, many renal patients just give up; they eat and drink whatever they want.

In these cases, dialysis is unable to achieve goal weight; and lab values of potassium, sodium, and phosphorous soar. We learned that dialysis was for survival, not normalcy.

It was very tempting to eat and drink what I wanted, knowing that a typical dialysis procedure would remove 8–9 pounds of fluid. I remember one lady who walked into dialysis carrying a large drink, which should have been her entire fluid budget for the day. She drank the whole 48 ounces during dialysis.

There is ample reason to stay on the renal diet. High potassium levels cause irregular heartbeats and sudden cardiac arrest. Elevated phosphorus values lead to calcium and phosphorus deposits in the heart, skin, lungs, and blood vessels, which cause heart attacks, bone disease, uncontrollable itching, and increased risk of death. Abnormal sodium and fluid levels create elevated blood pressure and increasing kidney damage.[36]

Dialysis patients have two types of body weight: fluid and dry. Fluid weight is the weight gained between dialysis treatments. Since there is little or no urine produced to remove extra fluid, *all* consumed fluids add to body weight. There is no cheating. Dry weight is achieved when blood pressure is controlled and there is no excess fluid, which is obtained after successful dialysis. The patient weighs before and after each dialysis to determine if ideal dry weight has been reached.

Symptoms of excessive fluid gain are high blood pressure, shortness of breath, and swelling. The patient will experience cramps, dizziness, headaches, and nausea during dialysis.[37] Paul was familiar with all these unpleasant symptoms from the hospital and did everything he could to prevent a reoccurrence.

Because diseased kidneys produce little to no urine, dialysis patients are often unable to void. Most people take this capacity for granted, but when there is no urine, there is no voiding. After Paul had been on dialysis for a few days, his urine output diminished to almost zero.

It was weird and something I never got used to. Like Forrest Gump, that's all I'm going to say about that.

AT LAST

We'd only been home two days, but it was crunch time for John Bolin, who was working nonstop on *Celebration*. He needed to know whose name to put on the program to sing "At Last." John e-mailed Paul to ask how he was doing; Paul called him to say that he was coming to the church that afternoon to "talk" about it.

Of course, that meant he was going to sing. John had absolutely no intention of Paul coming in, and I didn't think it was a great idea either, but Paul insisted. John needed a decision. Paul sang through the song at home raspy and weak, but got through it. I reluctantly drove him to church.

Jill Hofer, Houston First's Associate Director of Worship and gifted pianist, accompanied John and Paul while they sang. Paul sounded surprisingly good.

It was then that the words John had penned months earlier hit me full force. God used John long before these words would so dramatically impact my life. As I sang the final chorus, the words overcame me; I realized that God had performed another miracle, and he was receiving the glory.

A phrase in the chorus says, "I thought I'd never live to see this come to pass." There had definitely been days that I thought

I wouldn't live to sing again. From that moment on, every time I sang those words, I pictured myself in heaven, at Jesus's feet, just worshipping him.

John smiled. Jill and I wept. Paul said, "What?" And then, "I think it will work out." John said, "Good, because I already put your name in the program. Go home and rest your voice."

I thought there was no possible way for Paul to sing that solo, and yet hope was beginning to dawn. It wasn't just a song. It was the culmination of all the miracles that God had performed. It was a multitude of prayers being answered. It was obedience honored and God giving Paul his heart's desire. It was God's faithfulness highlighted in one man's harrowing walk from death's door to restored life. It was amazing. Simply amazing.

A few days later, just before Thanksgiving, I marveled again that God had spared Paul's life. In every crisis, God had provided a way out, a rescue. The orchestration of events that put us in the right place at the right time and with the right people had made *all* the difference—the difference between life and death.

I wasn't praying at the time, but God spoke to my heart with words that humbled me beyond belief. "I spared him for you…because of your faithfulness." To utter these words seems presumptuous since I'm the one with such *little* faith. But I will not deny God's faithfulness and thank him every day for his merciful hand in our lives.

December 8 was *Celebration*'s opening night. John and Paul had agreed that he should only sing "At Last," not the entire eighteen-song concert. He could never have endured six grueling performances of the complete program. Another choir member performed the king's processional since Paul simply wasn't strong enough to handle the heavy robes. Although cardiac ejection fraction had improved slightly, the external defibrillator remained in place, and dialysis was still three times a week.

Dressed as a king and with an artificial beard that replaced the one that had been shaved, Paul did a magnificent job, but God received the glory. It was a wonderful testimony to his faithfulness. The entire choir and orchestra, as well as many in the audience, were aware of the truth found in the chorus's closing line: "I thought I'd never live to see this come to pass, but now, at last."

The first night went well, but just before Paul came on stage for the second performance, the thought occurred to me to pray, which I rarely do when he sings. Honestly, I usually just enjoy listening, but I decided that praying might be a good idea, all things considered.

Afterwards, he shared that just before he started singing, he realized that the only words he could remember were the first four, "I'm just a man…" It stopped him cold. I was praying with all my heart. It's frightening to be standing in front of thousands of people and not remember the words. But he'd been through far worse and waited for the next line to come. It did, and the song went off without a hitch.

HUNTING TRIP

Our son-in-law Rett Rabe had asked what he could do for Paul while he was in the hospital. Since Rett was a fellow hunter, I shared with him that Paul had sorely missed the deer hunting trip. In addition, I had promised to replace the hunting trip. In retrospect, that was a foolish promise because I had no way to make it happen.

Rett, on the other hand, could arrange it and did. He had said, "No problem," but I really didn't expect it to work out. Hunting leases are scheduled months, even years, in advance, and Rett and his group had already used their lease earlier in the fall.

Nevertheless, the two of them hunted over New Year's Eve weekend—the last days of the season. Paul shot an 8-point buck, something he hadn't done since high school, and proudly brought the meat home. They also shot at squirrels and soda bottles and had a splendid manly time.

The best thing about the trip was being able to spend time with Rett. The rest was just icing on the cake. Although I was extremely disappointed about not going hunting in November, God had once again protected me. If I had been on that hunting trip, I would have died.

PART THREE:
TRANSPLANT

QUALIFYING

We returned to the cardiologist's office during the first week of 2012, fully expecting that the electrocardiogram (EKG) and echocardiogram would reveal an improved ejection fraction. Although it had earlier improved to 30–35 percent, it was stuck there and showed no further improvement.

This was a terribly discouraging day and placed all our hopes of kidney transplant in jeopardy. We had looked upon dialysis as temporary, expecting a prompt transplant. Now it appeared that God not only misunderstood our timetable, *he didn't even know the plan!*

At the end of the day, we had to acknowledge that God knew all about our future and our fears. We made a deliberate decision to put everything in his hands and praise him for it all. It's all we knew to do.

An appointment with Paul's nephrologist a few weeks later proved much more encouraging. He thought Paul was *ready for transplant* and would ask the St. Luke's kidney transplant team to start the evaluation process even though we didn't have cardiac clearance. This was very positive!

One of the reasons we tried so hard to facilitate the transplant before November was insurance related. We were slated to lose COBRA coverage from my former job in January 2012. This was a huge consideration since renal transplants cost over $200,000.

Unbeknownst to us, Medicare was available to kidney failure patients, even those under sixty-five. The national End Stage Renal Disease Program—Public Law 92-601— was passed in 1972 as an amendment to the Medicare Act and provided medical coverage to those who needed dialysis and/or renal transplant.[38] On February 1, 2012, at fifty-four years of age, Paul became Medicare eligible. It provided lifetime coverage for dialysis and thirty-six months coverage after transplant.

Insurance was one of my biggest fears. Having COBRA coverage for eighteen months, the Texas State Pool Insurance during January, and then becoming Medicare-eligible in February was amazing. To God be the glory.

On March 1, Paul was officially placed on the kidney transplant list, pending cardiology approval. This was just another step in the process, but it was a big step. Donor testing could finally begin.

During our initial meeting with St. Luke's kidney team, we explained how I had received my new liver within twenty-four days of being listed. This was nothing short of a miracle, and I knew it; but since we were bringing our own donor, we challenged them with a one-month timeline. Complete the donor testing and put us on the surgical schedule within thirty-one days, and we'd sing their praise. Our coordinators laughed, but we were serious.

DONOR EVALUATION

I always knew that my kidney would be compatible. Why wouldn't it? Sometimes you just know, even when there's no reason to know. I knew, and I was ready.

The decision to donate my kidney was an easy one. I wanted—and needed—Paul to survive. If a kidney was needed, I had an extra one. I knew there would be recuperation. I knew there was a small chance of complications. That was okay. Paul's life was worth the risk.

I was amazed at our friends' and family's reactions when told of our plan. Responses ranged from total surprise to outright disapproval. There was a litany of objections.

"What if something bad happens?"

"Can you live with just one kidney?"

"Will you have to take medication?"

"What about your grandchildren?"

"What does Paul say about this?"

"Are you sure? Really?"

These were valid questions, and they had good answers. Although surgeons never offer guarantees, donor risks are minimal. One kidney is sufficient, and in fact, the remaining one increases in size to take over the work of two. No long term medications would be required, and I had every intention of watching our grandchildren grow up. Paul was initially reluctant but then caved in. I was *very* sure.

Potential donors undergo thorough testing to verify that they are appropriate surgical candidates. Prevention of donor complications is vital. Certainly, the donor wishes to avoid problems, but so does the recipient since the donor is often family or friend. The professional reputation and financial backing of the transplant organization is dependent upon the success of each and every surgery, so they do everything feasibly possible to prevent complications.

Donors and recipients have separate coordinators who are responsible for evaluation, the waiting list, transplant preparation, and post-transplant management. Each coordinator keeps the best interests of their respective patient at the forefront of all planning.

Kidney transplants involving live donors are more advantageous than transplants using deceased donors. The living donor's kidney typically functions better, faster, and has a longer life span. Surgery can be scheduled, avoiding the uncertainty, stress, and three-to-five-year wait time for a cadaver kidney. Living donations can prevent the need for dialysis and kidney failure complications. Even so, two-thirds of donated kidneys are derived from deceased donors.[39]

Not everyone can be a living donor, but many can. Although individual transplant centers place varying emphasis on certain requirements, the most common are listed below.

Living donors must

- be eighteen years of age or older;
- not have uncontrolled hypertension, diabetes, HIV, sickle-cell disease, hepatitis B, malignancy, or infection;
- be in good general health, with acceptable kidney function;
- have acceptable anatomy for donation;
- not be pregnant;
- understand the risks, benefits, and complications associated with donation;
- be willing to donate a kidney without monetary gain or psychological coercion;
- have a compatible blood and tissue type as the recipient.

Compatible Blood Types	
Recipient's Blood Type	Donor's Blood Type
O	O
A	A or O
B	B or O
AB	A, B, AB or O

Donor evaluation consists of the following:

- Living Donor Coordinator Consult—this informs the potential donor about kidney donation and the transplant process.
- Nephrology Consult—the renal specialist assesses kidney function and donation safety.
- Transplant Surgeon—the surgeon discusses the appropriateness of kidney donation, risk of surgery, and possible complications.
- Social Worker Consult—a psychosocial assessment evaluates a potential donor's readiness.
- Registered Dietician Consult—the dietician assesses nutrition and provides education.
- Health exam

  ○ Laboratory testing screens immunity for viruses. Blood and urine tests determine if all organs, including the kidneys, are healthy.
  ○ A chest x-ray identifies lung problems.
  ○ An electrocardiogram assesses heart function.
  ○ A CT scan examines the abdomen and pelvis, determining which kidney is best for donation. (The left is preferred.)
  ○ A Pap smear and mammogram for women over forty evaluates presence of malignancies.
  ○ A PSA for men over fifty assesses prostate health.[40]

Donor kidneys can be removed either laparoscopically or by open nephrectomy. Laparoscopic surgery is a less invasive procedure in which the surgeon places two or three small holes in the donor's abdomen for a camera and surgical instruments; a larger incision (about four inches) is made for kidney removal. This method has better cosmetic results, requires fewer pain medications, and ensures a more rapid return to normal activities, usually three to four weeks.[41]

Pneumoperitoneum is a procedure used in laparoscopic surgeries whereby carbon dioxide gas is pumped into the abdomen. The gas distends the abdominal wall, which allows visualization and space to safely perform the procedure. Although necessary, this technique is the cause of residual abdominal gas, which causes postoperative discomfort.[42]

Donor anatomy or surgical history may necessitate an open nephrectomy. This surgery requires a larger incision in the flank area. Greater pain and longer recovery, typically four to six weeks, are associated with this procedure.[43]

The donor is not adversely affected by the loss of a kidney. People who have one kidney live just as long as those who have two.[44] A common misconception is that since we have two kidneys, we are carrying around a spare, like an extra tire, in case something happens to the other. That's not the way it works. If one kidney fails, the other one fails along with it.[45] We've either got two healthy kidneys or two unhealthy ones. There's no reason to hold on to the extra one.

Following surgery, the remaining kidney grows slightly larger and takes over the work of both kidneys. After surgical recuperation, the donor continues to live a normal life. There are no new medications or physical limitations.

Potential surgical risks include pain, infection, pneumonia, kidney damage, blood clotting, collapsed lung, anesthesia reaction, and bleeding. Kidney donation mortality is very rare—0.06 percent or about one death for every 1,700 procedures.[46] In comparison, the 2007 U.S. Census noted that infant mortality was 0.64 percent or sixty-four in ten thousand. Translation: it is twenty times more risky to be an infant in the United States than to donate a kidney.[47]

Donors and recipients do not have to be related. A living donor can be

- a family member, friend, spouse, or coworker;
- a directed altruistic donor (someone who donates a kidney to a person he knows);
- a non-directed altruistic donor (someone who donates a kidney to a nonspecific person on the waiting list); or
- a donor through the Paired Donor Exchange program. This person is willing to donate but is incompatible to the intended recipient. Many transplant programs offer the donor and recipient

an opportunity to match one incompatible donor/recipient pair to another pair who are incompatible. In other words, two donors donate to the other's recipient who is a match.[48]

The cost of renal donor evaluation is usually paid by the recipient's insurance, so there is no cost to the donor. However, the donor is not reimbursed for missed work days, travel, or lodging. Donors should investigate whether a short-term disability policy would be of benefit.[49]

Several friends and family members volunteered to be Paul's donor. Their honest willingness to be tested was a testimony to their sacrificial love and was appreciated beyond words. If I weren't a match, we would have to explore those options.

But I was the obvious first choice. I had blood type O, which is the universal donor. I met all requirements. If complications ensued, I wouldn't be leaving young children. Most importantly, I was extremely motivated; I wanted Paul well, and I was more than willing to sacrifice a kidney to make that happen.

Testing began with my gynecologist for an updated Pap smear and mammogram. Extensive lab work was taken on *multiple* occasions to check, recheck, and triple-check results. A chest x-ray showed no anomalies, and the EKG was normal. The nephrologist confirmed that my kidney was suitable for donation after an abdominal CT scan and twenty-four-hour urine collection.

Normal donor blood pressure is important. Fortunately, I had been a dedicated walker for many years and had logged literally thousands of miles. Although I was no athlete, the walking that I'd started while in my twenties contributed to my low blood pressure.

Seven different interviews were conducted by the transplant team. Nurses, social workers, and a dietician covered financial, psychological, emotional, and physical issues. The goal was to make certain that I was a suitable candidate and would be unlikely to suffer complications.

Although I was not symptomatic, the CT scan revealed gallstones, and my gastroenterologist ordered an abdominal ultrasound. It confirmed that my gallbladder was full of stones. He recommended that I have a cholecystectomy (gall bladder removal) either before or soon after the kidney surgery. I decided to defer this procedure since I wasn't having symptoms.

Because of an increased risk of blood clots, my gynecologist advised me to discontinue Premarin, which helps with menopausal symptoms, until after the surgery. That meant a return of hot flashes and night sweats. Great.

I had a long conversation with nephrology transplant surgeon Dr. Stephen Katz, who would perform my procedure. He confirmed that I wanted to donate a kidney and detailed exactly how he would remove it.

After signing all the consent papers, I had two requests if there were unforeseen complications, and I did not survive surgery: (1) Paul must receive my kidney and (2) all other usable organs should be donated.

Dr. Katz explained that I should tell my family about these wishes since they would be the decision-makers. I replied that I had already told my sister and daughter, but that since Paul would likely be anesthetized, I wanted him to know as well. I didn't want any confusion. He understood but said that he'd performed over three hundred nephrectomies with no major complications and didn't anticipate any problems. I said, "That's good, because I have three grandchildren that I want to see grow up." I was now ready.

Donor testing is not for the faint of heart. Whatever the transplant team wanted me to do, I did. I communicated at every conversation that I was ready to go. I was determined not to be the cause for delay. Early on, a kidney team member had commented that the donor sets the schedule. If the donor is slow to respond, the timetable drags. If the donor pushes, the process moves forward. I took this tidbit to heart and decided to push at every opportunity. I'm certain that it helped.

Paul had already completed similar tests and interviews. His surgeons were Drs. Charles Van Buren and Jacqueline Lappin. Dr. Van Buren performed the first Houston liver transplant in 1985 and was the associate director of the Division of Immunology and Organ Transplantation, Baylor College of Medicine (BCM) in Houston. Dr. Lappin was a BCM associate professor of surgery and surgical director of the pancreas transplant program. These surgeons had a vast amount of experience and were highly credentialed in the transplant community. We were extremely fortunate.

After all of my tests were completed (except the crossmatching), our case was presented to the transplant board on March 14. We were literally waiting with bated breath.

SECOND MATCH

There were three major hurdles that had to be cleared in order to be declared a compatible donor.

Number 1: Overall good health. √
Number 2: Blood compatibility. √
Number 3: Crossmatch testing. This was far more difficult and crucial.

The history of the term "match" is derived from the process of comparing human leukocyte antigens (HLA) in donors and recipients. Before the introduction of anti-rejection drugs, all six antigens of a recipient and donor had to "match" in order for the transplant to be successful. Now that these drugs have proven effective, HLA matching is not a factor in determining compatibility. Paul and I had no matching HLAs, which came as no surprise since we weren't related.

It's easier to describe the recipient and donor evaluation process using the terms "suitable" and "compatible," rather than "matching." A suitable donor is someone that is healthy enough to donate to anyone. A compatible donor is someone who, after passing a battery of compatibility assessment tests, is able to donate to the specific, intended recipient. There's a big difference.

Crossmatching is a sensitive and final test performed on both donor and recipient. This is the test that determines compatibility. It involves mixing cells and serum of both individuals to determine whether or not the recipient will reject the transplanted organ. The crossmatch is either positive or negative. A positive crossmatch means that the recipient has responded to the donor and that the transplant should *not* be carried out because of rejection risk. A negative crossmatch means that the recipient has not responded to the donor and that transplantation should be safe.[51]

The critical measure of crossmatching involves the recipient's panel-reactive antibodies (PRA), which is a blood test that measures the level of antibodies in the recipient's blood. The more antibodies present, the more difficult it is to find a compatible donor. A person's PRA can be anywhere from 0 percent to 99 percent and represents the percent of the United States population that the recipient's antibodies would react negatively to. A reaction would cause kidney rejection. For example, if Paul's PRA was 25, that would mean that 25 percent of the population would *not* be compatible donors.

About 20 percent of those who need a kidney transplant have high PRAs, meaning that their potential donor pool is limited. Because of this, transplants involving PRA's over

70 percent are unusual. These high PRAs develop as a result of blood transfusion, previous transplant, or pregnancy.

Unbelievably, studies showed that Paul had a PRA of 91 percent. This was unusually high because of accumulated antibodies from the previously transplanted liver and six blood transfusions. That created eight sets of antibodies (including Paul's original set) that had to be compatible to mine.

Lily Tovar, my donor coordinator, explained Paul's 91 percent like this: if there were one hundred potential donors *who had been cleared for surgery and had compatible blood types,* only nine would be acceptable. The other ninety-one would be incompatible because of antibodies. Against all odds, *I was one of the nine.* I always knew that I was a match, but I couldn't have imagined how unlikely it would be.

There was, however, one set of antibodies that strongly clashed. This was a significant problem. Although it did not prevent me from donating my kidney, it meant aggressive immunosuppression and five plasmapheresis procedures postoperatively for Paul.

Plasmapheresis, also known as therapeutic plasma exchange, is a blood purification procedure. Antibodies are proteins that circulate in the blood until they bind with the target tissue. Once bound, they impair the function of the target. Plasmapheresis removes antibodies from the blood, thus preventing an attack.

The process consists of blood removal, separation of blood cells from plasma, and return of these blood cells to the body's circulation. During the course of a single session, two to three liters (one-half to three-fourths gallon) of plasma are removed and replaced. It is similar to dialysis and, of course, requires a central line.[51]

Although the plasmapheresis procedures would add to Paul's postoperative regimen, they wouldn't prevent the transplant. The important thing was that we matched. Again. Now all we needed was cardiac clearance.

GOOD ENOUGH!

Agonizing dread, along with hopeful anticipation, intensified until our March cardiologist appointment. If the echocardiogram didn't show significant improvement, all hopes of transplant were off, at least for the foreseeable future. We were so scared.

As we sat in the examining room waiting for echocardiogram results, it dawned on me that waiting for Paul's heart function to normalize was simply protection against perioperative disaster, in other words, death on the operating table. We shouldn't try to talk Dr. Feghali into something that would be detrimental in the long run, as if we could sway him! This helped calm my fears. Dialysis was far better than death on the table.

An associate physician whom we'd never seen before came in to review Paul's medical history. We were more than a little annoyed at the wait. Then he blandly said that the echocardiogram was *normal*. In unison, we cried out, "What?" (We rarely hear that word applied to Paul.)

He repeated himself, and Paul asked, "What was the number?" The associate said he didn't know the exact number but that he looked at the echocardiogram, and it was normal. More forceful than I think he realized, Paul said, "Well, go out and look at the number!"

So he did. Coming back with Dr. Feghali, he reported that the number was 45 percent. From 30 to 35 percent in January to *45 percent* in March! He said it so calmly, but to us, it was the difference between life and death. It was a chance for real life versus a few years of dialysis survival then succumbing to cardiovascular complications or infection.

We were ecstatic and gave all glory to God! Dr. Feghali went on to say that Paul's heart was normalizing and might continue to improve. Regardless, he was now a surgical candidate!

Dr. Feghali said, "Your heart function isn't normal, but it's good enough." Those words were sweet music to my ears. I'll take "good enough."

We reported the cardiac results by e-mail to our prayer warriors. Cardiologist friend Dr. Dale Faulkner commented, "You know, since this is my business, I feel like I have to say something. What happened to Paul *just doesn't* happen, not after five months." We were so ignorant of heart and kidney issues, we operated simply by faith, trusting God to help us through desperate times. There were so many miracles.

The Transplant Board was scheduled to meet on March 21 to discuss cardiac clearance, antibody studies, postoperative immunosuppression, liver issues, and the final verdict on my donor compatibility.

We received final transplant approval on March 23, with surgery scheduled for March 30. Lily, my coordinator, asked if we were still okay with that date, and I said, "Yes! We're ready!"

March 30—thirty days from being listed. They had met the timeline challenge with one day to spare! We couldn't have been more pleased.

POLISH VISITOR AND TOOTHACHE

When the transplant was more of a dream than real hope, I had invited a young Polish friend to spend time with us. Katarzyna Rumin (Kasia) was a foreign exchange student from Warsaw who had spent nine months with Cindy and me during their senior year of high school. That was 2000–2001, and Kasia hadn't been back since then.

She bought airline tickets in January, asking if March 21–April 8 would be a good time. I e-mailed her back that although we hoped that a kidney transplant was in Paul's future, I had no reason to expect that those dates would present a problem. I told her to buy the tickets and come on!

I was thrilled that Kasia was returning to the United States and we had a tearful reunion. Since leaving twelve years before, she had graduated from college in Warsaw, was advancing her career, and had moved into a new apartment. She is an amazing young woman, and I am so proud of her.

So it was that the week before transplant was spent with Kasia. She was a wonderful companion and a gift from God. She planned to visit a San Francisco friend from March 31 to April 8, which was perfect timing. Since the surgeries were planned for the thirtieth, Kasia spent the last two days with Cindy, who also took her to the airport.

Surgery was scheduled for Friday. Sharon had a toothache over the weekend, so our dentist, Dr. Chris Gowan, graciously made time to see her on Monday. To be on the safe side, he referred her to an endodontist to confirm that a tiny crack in a back molar could be addressed after surgery. None of us wanted that tooth to abscess and prevent the surgeries. They both concurred, and we were still a go!

ROBUST KIDNEY

March 30 finally arrived. After all the hoping, praying, waiting, and testing—it was finally time. We had to be at the hospital by 5:30 a.m., but getting ready didn't take long since I couldn't wear makeup and we couldn't eat breakfast!

On the way to the medical center, Sharon mentioned that after this was over, she wanted to become involved in kidney transplants. Laughing, I said, "Honey, you're about as involved as you can get. You're giving one today." But that wasn't what she meant. She wanted to encourage future kidney donors, which is why we wrote this book.

We found the preop nurses' station and started the admitting process. It was the same sixth-floor unit that Paul had been in, five months earlier. They put us in a room together, which seems like a no-brainer but was actually a result of our friend, Joy, calling the night before. They were expecting us. More blood was drawn, if you can believe it, more consent papers were signed, and the horrible hospital gowns were donned.

Our son Jason had accompanied us to the hospital, but more family soon arrived. We visited and prayed with Paul's siblings and parents, each of whom whispered heartfelt gratitude for donating my kidney. Around the time we were supposed to head to the operating room, the nurse reported a delay.

A recent kidney recipient required a revision, a rare complication. This bumped us to second place, so we waited another hour. They came for me at 9:30 a.m., and Paul gave me a sweet kiss before they wheeled me out. I had decided months ago to approach this surgery unafraid, so I refused to explore the "what-if" scenarios. We had been pushing for these surgeries for seven months. I wasn't going to get sappy now! They let my sister, Cynthia, go with me. That was good. I wasn't nervous, but it was nice to have someone along.

This was when it hit me full force. Sharon was putting her life on the line for me. Her surgeon, Dr. Stephen Katz, came back to meet me in the preop area. Grabbing his hand and pulling him close, I softly told him that there were hundreds of people praying for him today. I also told him that he had my entire life in his hands during Sharon's surgery and to please treat it well.

I had told John Bolin that if for some reason I didn't survive surgery, he and Dennis were to perform the most celebratory funeral anyone had ever seen. God was to get all the glory. I wanted to make sure the opportunity was used to present the Gospel in a captivating way. My prayer was that many people would come to know Christ.

In the holding area, there were more interviews with the anesthesiologist and circulating nurse. I again confirmed that I wanted to donate my kidney. If a donor has second thoughts or concerns, there are *ample* opportunities to reconsider. I was so ready; I must have seemed an idiot. All questions had been answered long ago, and I had no reservations.

My one request to the circulating nurse was for as much dignity as possible. Throughout my nursing career, I'd visited the operating room on numerous occasions and had witnessed many instances of needless patient exposure. A person is never more vulnerable than when anesthetized. This haunted me, and she knew exactly what I meant. She assured me that she would personally do everything possible to keep me draped. I appreciated this and asked for nothing else.

Paul went to the operating room at 10:00 a.m. and went through the same procedures. Throughout our surgeries, friends and family prayed. They prayed for the surgeons, anesthesiologists, nurses, technicians, and us.

Paul's new kidney was placed on the lower right side of his abdomen and then surgically connected to nearby blood vessels. The ureter was attached to the bladder to allow for urine passage. Diseased kidneys are usually left intact unless there have been repeated infections, uncontrolled hypertension, or backup of urine into the kidneys. Any of these scenarios would put the new kidney at risk. None applied to Paul, so his original kidneys were left in place; he now had three.

The surgeons reported that the new kidney produced urine within two minutes of being connected. By 4:30 p.m., we were both safely in cardiovascular ICU/recovery.

Dr. Van Buren described the transplanted kidney as "robust," and the name stuck. We often affectionately talk about our "robust kidney." Dr. Katz reported that he had carefully inspected Sharon's gallbladder and found no inflammation or external indication of stones. I was grateful that we had not delayed the transplant to have it removed.

We were in separate recovery/ICU rooms. I was in a ward with five other new surgical patients; because of his immunosuppressed status, Paul was in a private room with foldout glass doors. After I spent a few hours in the recovery room, I was moved to a different ICU ward for overnight observation, but there was a slight detour.

Our nurse friend who worked at the hospital, Joy Lasco, knew that we desperately wanted to see each other. Even if someone reports that so-and-so is doing just fine, you need to see with your own eyes that all is well. I certainly did. Joy swept into my little cubicle and asked if I wanted to see Paul. I responded with a resounding, "Yes!" And as if they did this every day, she said, "Let's go!"

With my nurse's permission, Joy unhooked monitors, released the brakes, and pushed me down the corridor toward the private rooms. Just so you know, the private rooms are spacious, but they are definitely meant for only one bed. There were IV poles everywhere and all sorts of monitoring devices attached to Paul. He was positioned in the middle of the room, with little space left for me. That did not deter Joy.

With the help of his nurse, she unfolded and opened the entire glass door, rearranging the room so that my bed could be squeezed in. This was no small feat, but knowing how important it was to us, she persevered. She put our beds side by side and closed the glass doors for privacy. Our daughter Lindsay happened to be there and took a picture on her cell phone.

We were together for only about twenty minutes before they moved me to a separate room, but it was so good to see each other. Paul's color was already pink instead of the pale gray to which I'd become accustomed during his months on dialysis. We held hands and praised God for his mercy.

One of Sharon's prayers was that we would be able to share a hospital room. Although that didn't work out, we were able to share the preop room and an ICU room, if only for a brief time. God is so good. Seeing her was the best thing in the world for me. What a blessing!

Everyone on the transplant team had warned that my recuperation would be longer and more difficult than Paul's. I frankly didn't believe them. How could that be true? They were just going to take out one little kidney; grafting it into Paul was much more difficult. Nevertheless, I soon discovered that they were right.

Although he was moving tentatively, Paul was soon up walking. He felt much better than I did and required fewer pain medications. The steroids that were given as part of the immunosuppression regimen reduced inflammation and thus reduced postoperative pain.

On the other hand, my pain was unrelenting, and the intravenous Dilaudid was ineffective. While there were frequent fifteen-minute intervals of unconsciousness, my wakeful time was spent in pain. In order to assess pain level, nurses frequently asked, "Where is your pain on a scale of 1–10?" During the first few days, it hovered between 8 and 9.

I should have switched to another pain medication, as Dr. Van Buren recommended, but I thought it would get better. It didn't. This is when patients need knowledgeable advocates to help make decisions for them. The problem was that my advocate had just had surgery himself and was isolated in ICU.

Two days after the surgery, I switched to Buprenex injections every six hours. This brought the pain level down from 8 to 4 and was much better. By the next day, I had switched to oral Vicodin. In the meantime, I developed nightmares and hallucinations.

I remembered Paul's terrible mental changes in November and resolved to take only Tylenol from then on. I couldn't deal with delirium. From April 4, I relied solely on Tylenol for pain relief. As time progressed, it became obvious that this was not a good plan.

ONE MORE

Two days after surgery Paul developed a complication that required surgical revision. Since he was doing so well, the urinary catheter was removed prematurely, creating swelling and a kinked ureter. (The ureter is the tube that connects the kidney to the bladder.) The kink prevented him from voiding, which was a huge problem. His urine output deteriorated from normal to nonexistent.

I was heartsick about this development, but there was simply no other option: he had to go back to surgery. Paul was relieved that decisive action was being taken. The new kidney was at risk. Knowing that something was wrong, he had proactively decided not to eat or drink anything all day. If he hadn't done this, we would have had to wait much longer for surgery. The decision was made at 12:30 p.m., and he was back in the operating room by 1:15 p.m.

Dr. Lappin reopened the recent incision, inspected everything, and repaired the kink. An hour and a half later, Paul was back in the cardiovascular ICU where he spent the night. Since he was being given declining doses of steroids, his pain was more intense after the second surgery than the first.

While waking up from anesthesia in the operating room, I realized that one of the assisting surgeons was reinserting the Foley catheter. Since it can be uncomfortable and embarrassing, they typically do this while anesthetized. It hurt like a big dog, and I let her know it! Now whenever she sees me, she asks if I've forgiven her. Nah!

We were on different hospital floors. Since Paul was extremely immunosuppressed, he was confined to the transplant floor. I was a typical surgical patient and had been placed elsewhere. Going from floor to floor was painful, and not seeing each other regularly made my recuperation more stressful.

Visits from family and friends eased the strain. After leaving ICU, Cindy and Cynthia took turns spending the first seventy-two hours with me, which helped tremendously. Lindsay and Kristen, as well as other family and friends, checked on us often.

The same central line that had been used for Paul's dialysis was utilized for the series of five plasmapheresis procedures. Along with aggressive immunosuppressive medications and steroids, the antibody disparity was kept in check.

I thought that my days of using the dialysis catheter were over. Disappointed when I woke up and found it intact, I later realized that it would be used for plasmapheresis. Then I was glad it was there; it wasn't discontinued for another three weeks.

I was discharged from the hospital after six days but didn't want to go home without Paul. I just couldn't. So I spent two nights at Cindy's, who lived nearby, until Paul's release.

Paul's creatinine levels steadily declined from over 9 to an amazing 1.2. He hadn't seen a creatinine level that low for many years. That little number was why he needed a kidney and why I had given him mine. It's a wonderful number.

After a lengthy discussion about the new immunosuppression regimen, Paul was discharged the next day. We were moving slowly, but at least we were moving.

The transplant bell is a twelfth-floor tradition. Mounted on the wall by the elevator, it looks like a ship's bell. Every new organ transplant recipient rings the bell just before going home. A nearby plaque says,

> "Ring this bell three times well; toll to clearly say.
> My transplant's done; the course is run."

We stood side by side and thanked God for the opportunity to ring that bell. Surviving the November crises had required God's supernatural intervention. Today was no different, and multiple miracles had made this day possible.

- Written months before, the lyrics to "At Last" perfectly highlighted Paul's survival.

- Although released from the hospital just two weeks earlier, he was able to sing in *Celebration*.
- Transplant insurance issues were resolved so that we were responsible for only $1,200 of the $200,000 hospital bill.
- We waited only thirty days between when Paul was listed and the actual surgeries.
- Even though Paul had a very high antibody level, I was a compatible donor.
- After five months of heart failure, his ejection fraction returned to an acceptable 45 percent.
- Although my tooth had a tiny crack, there was no infection, and surgery could proceed.
- All three surgeries were successful!

Two days later, Paul sent this e-mail:

Dearest family & friends,

To God be the glory! We are so thankful to our faithful prayer warriors. We know God has heard your prayers. He has and will sustain us through this trial. We praise God for what he has already done and wait faithfully for what he has for us in the future.

While I am grateful for your prayers, I am most thankful to Sharon who gladly gave of herself to give me another chance at life. It is a great parallel of how Christ gave himself for us. I am forever in her debt, a debt which I can never repay.

Please continue to pray for us during recovery, specifically for strength and no infections. I am at the most immunosuppressed state I have ever been and am very vulnerable to germs and sickness.

We love you all and hope to see everyone soon.

Blessings,
Paul

TRULY THANKFUL

I'd like to be able to say that my recovery was quick and relatively painless, but it wasn't. I thought the pain would rapidly subside, and I'd turn the corner when I got home, but that corner turned out to be very elusive. Surgery is surgery, and recuperation takes time. There was a constant burn around the incision, feeling like a stomach virus. Intestinal bubbles hurt the incision area, and residual abdominal gas caused shoulder pain.

The pain was still problematic after two weeks. At our first follow-up appointment, Dr. Lappin decided to "break the pain cycle" and anesthetized my entire abdomen by injecting multiple doses of Lidocaine. This provided temporary relief. She strongly suggested that I take a stronger pain medication for a few days. I agreed, and it helped. My Tylenol-only plan was ditched.

My mom, Faye Anderson, was our guardian angel. She brought food and checked on us every day. Four weeks and three days postoperatively, I woke up and felt 100 percent better. I felt good again.

Ten weeks after our surgeries, Gregg Matte, pastor of Houston's First Baptist Church, started a six-week series on *Real Life, Real People*. He asked if Paul and I were willing to share our story during all three services. We were to highlight the first topic in the series—marriage.

Paul had promised God in November, when he was fighting for every breath, that he would share his story if he survived, so we readily agreed. Sitting on stage in front of hundreds of people, Gregg asked about past medical crises and how God had used them in our lives. Paul gave a brief synopsis and told how it had strengthened our marriage and faith.

Gregg noted, "It costs most people an arm and a leg when they get married, but in your case, it cost a kidney. A kidney! How does that make you feel, Sharon?"

I replied that giving up my kidney was an easy decision because Paul had laid down his life for me first. He loves me every day, just like Christ loves the church. Being so loved, what *wouldn't* I do for him?

We're just ordinary people and give God glory for everything that has happened. It seemed strange for us to be the ones talking about marriage since both of us had chosen poorly when we were young. But we were proof that God can redeem his own if they give him the opportunity.

I am much closer to the Lord and to Sharon because God graciously allowed me to go through so many health issues. The journey has been worth it.

Many believe that donors are noble and self-sacrificing. I was, in fact, labeled heroic, courageous, and even saintly! Not so. I gave my kidney to Paul for one reason and one reason only: I wanted him to survive. I wanted us to grow old together. One little kidney was a small price to pay for that potential privilege.

People who know our story often ask, "How is Paul?" It's a difficult question because we are *always* juggling various health concerns. Transplants don't come without ongoing follow-up, medication changes, and exhaustive testing. It's a trade-off from the original disease to immunosuppression disease. Transplants don't erase medical problems; they just offer potential.

However, let me reassure you, Paul is well. God has sustained his life against all odds and blessed us immeasurably. We are truly thankful.

As you might have guessed, Paul and I are passionate advocates of organ donation, both living and deceased. But here are the undeniably brutal facts:

- 96,103 people are currently listed for a kidney transplant.
- Many wait over five years for a deceased kidney donor.
- A staggering 4,500 Americans die every year waiting for a kidney.[52]

If you are in good health, you could very well be a suitable donor. If you are not in good health, some organs might be acceptable for donation after your death. Please consider both options and talk to your family about your decision. *Thank you.*

EPILOGUE

Just before the book was printed I received an amazing email from Kasia, my Polish friend. Raised in the Roman Catholic faith, she did not have a personal relationship with Christ. She struggled to understand or accept that God loved her and had a plan for her life. There was a disconnect between her heart and faith in Christ. When she and I talked about Jesus, she simply could not let go of her unbelief. But that changed.

In late March 2013, Kasia, her boss and a co-worker went on a business trip to Kiev, Ukraine. In her own words, "The most unbelievable thing that I've ever experienced has happened. My co-worker was actually a messenger from God. At first I didn't realize it and felt like he was just trying to motivate me to take responsibility for my life, to stop wasting time. It was good to talk to him even though deep inside I feared that what he was saying was impossible."

Continuing, she wrote, "The miracle happened in the plane while we were flying home to Warsaw. Somehow I just believed and trusted God because it seemed that there was nothing to lose. During our conversation, *I just let it all go*. The relief and freedom that had eluded me for so long were mine. Now I am light and happy for the first time in my life. My heart and soul were healed."

"It's a wonderful feeling as well as a great responsibility. Now there is much work to do! I love to think that I met God in 'heaven'. Back in church, it feels like I have returned home. It is truly unbelievable."

So…it doesn't matter if God meets your need in the elevator or on a plane, at home or in church. A changed heart is the greatest miracle of all!

INDEX

ENDNOTES

1   www.ccfa.org

2   www.patients.gi.org

3   www.digestive.niddk.nih.gov

4   www.stlukeshouston.com

5   http://www.elyrics.net/read/n/neil-diamond-lyrics/the-story-of-my-life-lyrics.html

6   www.medterms.com

7   http://www.transplantation-proceedings.org/article/S0041-1345(04)00084-3/abstract

8   www.kidney.org

9   www.kidney.org

10 www.bidmc.org

11 http://171.66.127.177/content/75/4/258.full

12 www.nhlbi.nih.gov

13 http://my.clevelandclinic.org

14 http://my.clevelandclinic.org

15 www.drcnh.org/restraint.pdf

16 http://emedicine.medscape.com/article/304068-overview#aw2aab6b7

17 http://en.wikipedia.org/wiki/Oxygen_therapy

18 Isaiah 55:9, NIV paraphrased

19 "Don't Let Me Miss the Glory" by Carl Cartee and Joe Beck

20 www.webmd.com

21 www.mayoclinic.com

22 Hebrews 13:5, NIV paraphrased

23 Lamentations 3:22-23, NIV paraphrased

24 www.ncbi.nlm.nih.gov

25 "Great Is Thy Faithfulness" is a hymn written by Thomas Chisholm (1866–1960); music composed by William M. Runyan (1870–1957).

26 I John 4:18 NIV

27 www.my.clevelandclinic.org

28 2 Corinthians 1:8-12, The Message

29 www.kidney.niddk.nih.gov

30 www.kidney.org

31 www.ncbi.nlm.nih.gov

32 www.kidney.org

33 www.unos.org

34 www.kidney.org

35 www.davita.com

36 www.davita.com

37 www.davita.com

38 www.mydd.com

39 www.livingdonorsonline.org

40 www.stlukeshouston.com

41 www.livingdonorsonline.org

42 www.laparoscopy.blogs.com

43 www.livingdonorsonline.org
44 www.kidneyregistry.org
45 www.sclerodermatt.org
46 www.kidney.org
47 www.kidneyregistry.org
48 www.livingkidneydonation.co.ukl
49 www.stlukeshouston.com
50 www.livingkidneydonorsnetwork.org
51 www.medical-dictionary.thefreedictionary.com
52 www.lkdn.org